A Map to the Next World

A Map to the Next World

Poetry and Tales

Joy Harjo

W. W. Norton & Company / New York / London

For more information about permission to reproduce selections from this book,
write to Permissions, W. W. Norton & Company, Inc., 500 Fifth Avenue,
New York, NY 10110

The text and display of this book are composed in Electra
Composition by Allentown Digital Services Division of R. R. Donnelley
& Sons Company
Manufacturing by Haddon Craftsmen
Book design by JAM Design

Library of Congress Cataloging-in-Publication Data

Harjo, Joy.
  A map to the next world : poetry and tales / Joy Harjo.
      p. cm.
  ISBN 0-393-04790-3
    I. Title.
  PS3558.A62423 M36 2000
  811'.54 21—dc21

                                                          99-041099

W. W. Norton & Company, Inc., 500 Fifth Avenue, New York, N.Y. 10110
www.wwnorton.com

W. W. Norton & Company Ltd., 10 Coptic Street, London WC1A 1PU

1 2 3 4 5 6 7 8 9 0

Contents

Acknowledgments

With gratitude to the Witter Bynner Foundation, the National Endowment for the Arts, the Lila Wallace Reader's Digest Fund, and the Native Writers Circle of the Americas. Your support matters.

Grateful acknowledgment to the publications where some of these poems and prose pieces appear, including *American Indian Culture & Research Journal, Scan, The A Book, The Atlantic Center for the Arts Publication*, and *The American Poetry Review*.

And thanks to the many whose kindnesses are crucial to the appearance of this collection:

Linda Alexander and Ted Isham for the Mvskoke translation and their dedication to the language.

Audrey Powers for use of her letter excerpt in "threads of blood and spirit."

Lily, Imelda, Erlinda and Angelica Cruz, my family in Laurel Canyon.

The insistent brown bird who accompanied me most mornings I wrote in that canyon.

For Vanessa, Natasha and Tamarin Chee, who inspire me with their drawings and poems.

For Krista Rae, Haleigh, Desiray, and Tayo, who will continue this path.

For Ratonia Haywood, a daughter in every sense of the word. And ongoing thanks to my son Phil and daughter Rainy. You are impetus for this work.

For the poets: Adrienne Rich, Mahmud Darwish, Roque Dalton and Luci Tapahonso.

For the warriors: Nusrat Fateh Ali Khan, Israel Kamakawiwo'ole, Ken Sarowiwo, and Ingrid Washinawatok. You continue to matter.

vkvsamet hesaketvmese pomvte
mowc towckvs pokvhoyen yiceyvte
mon vkerrickv heren
pohvkerricen vpeyeyvres

With praise for the Breathmaker through whose intent
we arrive here, and by whose grace we leave

for Lurline Wailana McGregor, pau ʻole

for Gregory M. Sarris, who stood by me through the difficult birth

Part I

Songline of Dawn

Songline of Dawn

We are ascending through the dawn
the sky blushed with the fever
                              of attraction.
I don't want to leave my daughter,
                              or the babies.
I can see their house, a refuge in the dark near the university.
Protect them, oh gods of the scarlet light
who love us fiercely despite our acts of stupidity
our utter failings.
May this morning light be food for their bones,
for their spirits dressed
                              in manes of beautiful black hair
in skins the color of the earth as it meets the sky.
Higher we fly over the valley of monster bones
left scattered in the dirt to remind us that breathing
is rooted somewhere other than the lungs.
                              My spirit approaches with reverence
because it harbors the story, of how these beloveds appeared to fail
then climbed into the sky to stars of indigo.
                              And we keep going past the laughter and tears
of the babies who will grow up to become a light field
just beyond us.
And then the sun breaks over the yawning mountain.
And the plane shivers as we dip toward
                              an old volcanic field.
It is still smoldering
motivated by the love of one deity for another.
It's an old story and we're in it so deep we have become them.
The sun leans on one elbow after making love,
                              savoring the wetlands just off the freeway.
We are closer to the gods than we ever thought possible.

the psychology of earth and sky

It is just before dawn. The mango tree responds to the wind's fierce jostling. A rooster stridently marks the emerging light. We are alerted and our spirits trek back through night and the stars to awaken here in this place known by *Honolulu*. Clouds harboring rain travel fast over the city and now a trash truck beeps as it backs up for collection. And dawn arrives, no matter the struggle of the night and how endless that night might be.

We are part of an old story and involved in it are migrations of winds, of ocean currents, of seeds, songs and generations of nations.

In this life it seems like I am always leaving, flying over this earth that harbors many lives. I was born Indian, female and artist in the Creek Nation. It is still grey out as I follow the outline of memory. Over there is my teenage self getting out of a car, still a little drunk, waving good-bye to friends. We've been up all night, singing into the dark, joining the stars out on the mesa west of the Indian town, Albuquerque.

"When the dance is over sweetheart I will take you home in my one-eyed Ford. Wey-yo-hey-ya Hey-yah-hah. Hey-yah-hah."

That song was destined to become a classic.

The shutting of the car door echoes and echoes and leads to here. I always hear that door when I return to that memory. It's a holographic echo, turning over and over into itself. I am leaving. I am returning.

I turned to walk to my apartment in the back. All of us lived in the back of somewhere in that city where we were defining what it meant to be Indian in a system of massive colonization. It was a standing joke. A backdoor joke. The world was suddenly condensed by the shutting of the door, the sweet purr of the engine as the car drove off and the perfect near silence of the pause in the morning scramble of sparrows, the oohhing of doves. I can still breathe it, that awareness of being alive part of the ceremony for the rising of the sun. I often lived for this moment of reconciliation, where night and morning met. It didn't matter that I didn't quite know how I was going to piece together what I needed for tuition, rent, groceries, books and childcare, how I was going to make sense of a past that threatened to destroy me during those times when I doubted that I deserved a place in the world. The songs we sang all night together filled me with promise, hope, the belief in a community that understood that the world was more than a contract between buyer and seller.

And that morning just as the dawn was arriving and I was coming home I knew that the sun needed us, needed my own little song made of the whirr push of the blood through my lungs and heart. Inside that bloodstream was born my son, my daughter. I was born of parents who would greet the dawn often in their courtship with their amazing passion driven by love, and later heartbreak.

Dawn was also the time my father often came home after he and my mother were married, had four children, dropped off by his friends, reeking of smoke, beer and strange perfume. And I am his daughter. How much do we have to say in the path our feet will take? Is it ordained by the curve of a strand of DNA? Mixed with the urge to love, to take flight? My family survived, even continues to thrive, which works against the myth of Indian defeat and disappearance.

My daughter's house is near the First National Bank building in Albuquerque, a landmark from the sky as I climb toward the dawn in a jet. She is still asleep, the youngest curled in her arms. Her oldest is sleeping with her mouth open next to the three other beauties who also call my daughter *mother*. Anytime I left as she was growing up she missed me terribly. Even now as I fly away from her yet once more I feel the tug of her heart as it still questions the time of my next return, as if I left her at some point in the deepest roots of her memory and never came back. I want to tell her I will never leave her, and I send this poem to her and the girls as a guardian spirit.

Instinct

In the dark I travel by instinct,
through the rubble of nightmares,
groaning of monsters toward the crack of light
along your body's horizon.
I roll over to my side, take you in my nostrils
test you for shape, intention and food
as nations fall apart.
Small winds tattoo my cheek.
Soon they will bring mist,
a small rain to clean the world
send rainbows to dress us,
for the ceremony
to rid us of the enemy mind.

when we were born we remembered everything

We are living in a system in which human worth is determined by money, material wealth, color of skin, religion and other capricious factors that do not tell the true value of a soul. This is an insane system. Those who profit from this system have also determined, by rationale and plundering, that the earth also has no soul, neither do the creatures, plants or other life forms matter. I call this system the *overculture*. There is no culture rooted here from the heart, or the need to sing. It is a system of buying and selling. Power is based on ownership of land, the work force, on the devaluation of life. The power centers are the multinational corporations who exploit many to profit a few. True power does not amass through the pain and suffering of others.

Phillip Deere, a spiritual leader from the Mvskoke, predicted the many twists and turns this path through the colonized world could take. He and others like him warned that this season will eventually pass, but not without great pain and suffering for everyone.

It's difficult to walk through the illusion without being awed and distracted by it. Power is seductive and sparkles. False gold also glitters. We think we know the difference, but it's easy to be seduced when all appearances tell you there is everything to be gained by winning.

At birth we know everything, can see into the shimmer of complexity. When a newborn looks at you it is with utter comprehension. We know where we are coming from, where we have been. And then we forget it all. That's why infants sleep so much after birth. It is an adjustment. The details of a new awareness have to be fine-tuned. But memory is elastic and nothing is ever forgotten. It's submerged below the bloodstream, in the river of memory informing us of direction, like a gyroscope in the heart of a ship. We are all headed to the same destination, eventually.

We who greet these arriving souls rejoice that the old ones have returned and will accompany us through the next cycle of the story.

I struggled and choked as I slid down the road through my mother. She was terrified, had no maternal instruction on birth. I wanted out as quickly as possible yet had serious doubts as to whether I wanted to take it on, a life that early on would run the jagged borders of despair and joy, so I went forwards and backwards, fought and nearly killed both of us as I came into this world, two months before my due date. I still battle impatience and the bad habit of struggle when there need be no fight.

I try to remember the beautiful sense of the pattern that was revealed before that first breath when the struggle in this colonized world threatens to destroy the gifts that my people carry into the world. But we cannot be destroyed. Destiny can be shifted by evil, but only for a little while.

A Map to the Next World

for Desiray Kierra Chee

In the last days of the fourth world I wished to make a map for those who would climb through the hole in the sky.

My only tools were the desires of humans as they emerged from the killing fields, from the bedrooms and the kitchens.

For the soul is a wanderer with many hands and feet.

The map must be of sand and can't be read by ordinary light. It must carry fire to the next tribal town, for renewal of spirit.

In the legend are instructions on the language of the land, how it was we forgot to acknowledge the gift, as if we were not in it or of it.

Take note of the proliferation of supermarkets and malls, the altars of money. They best describe the detour from grace.

Keep track of the errors of our forgetfulness; the fog steals our children while we sleep.

Flowers of rage spring up in the depression. Monsters are born there of nuclear anger.

Trees of ashes wave good-bye to good-bye and the map appears to disappear.

We no longer know the names of the birds here, how to speak to them by their personal names.

Once we knew everything in this lush promise.

What I am telling you is real and is printed in a warning on the map. Our forgetfulness stalks us, walks the earth behind us, leaving a trail of paper diapers, needles and wasted blood.

An imperfect map will have to do, little one.

The place of entry is the sea of your mother's blood, your father's small death as he longs to know himself in another.

There is no exit.

The map can be interpreted through the wall of the intestine—a spiral on the road of knowledge.

You will travel through the membrane of death, smell cooking from the encampment where our relatives make a feast of fresh deer meat and corn soup, in the Milky Way.

They have never left us; we abandoned them for science.

And when you take your next breath as we enter the fifth world there will be no X, no guidebook with words you can carry.

You will have to navigate by your mother's voice, renew the song she is singing.

Fresh courage glimmers from planets.

And lights the map printed with the blood of history, a map you will have to know by your intention, by the language of suns.

When you emerge note the tracks of the monster slayers where they entered the cities of artificial light and killed what was killing us.

You will see red cliffs. They are the heart, contain the ladder.

A white deer will come to greet you when the last human climbs from the destruction.

Remember the hole of our shame marking the act of abandoning our tribal grounds.

We were never perfect.

Yet, the journey we make together is perfect on this earth who was once a star and made the same mistakes as humans.

We might make them again, she said.

Crucial to finding the way is this: there is no beginning or end.

You must make your own map.

the appearance of the sacred was not likely

◎

In the months before the birth of my third granddaughter, a Navajo deity appeared to a blind woman who lived far away from the cities in a distant part of the reservation. This was an unusual occurrence, something unheard of in recent history. Such visits come about historically only in times of terrible stress, when people have lost the way. The deity explained that the people were in danger, and that unless they kept up the traditions that made them particularly Navajo, a complex and beautiful system of prayer and thanksgiving, they would suffer the loss of what makes them powerful in this world.

After this visit many people made pilgrimages to the old woman's hogan to see the place the deity stood, to hear the story once again and talk about it with each other. We who heard the story in Albuquerque talked about it, pondered it as we watched the kids' basketball games, ate dinner together, or dressed for work. We considered the meaning and timing of the appearance of this shimmering one, and wondered how it will continue to mean in this world apparently driven into craziness by violence and greed.

Though I am not Navajo I am related to many Navajos and two of my granddaughters and grandson are Navajo. I have been as influenced by Navajo thought as I have by European thought, though I am a Mvskoke. As a longtime resident of lands near one of the sacred mountains of the Navajo I too am affected by the shape and meaning of the deity and the message.

The deity's visitation occurred as my granddaughter Desiray was forming in her mother's belly. The event charged the atmosphere with nutrients, helped feed the growing child. When a woman is pregnant she must be careful about what she thinks, what she says and the kinds of places and people she is around. She is especially vulnerable, as is the child, to negativity of any kind.

It was not by accident that this granddaughter is born to us at this particular time. I see her as a link to the prophecy, one who came to us because of our love for this land, for the people. When she came into the world she was accompanied by the spirits of her father's great-grandmother, and my great-aunt.

This pregnancy was much more peaceful than my daughter's first. Desiray was born quickly and easily. So quick and easy that by the time my friend and I made it to the Bernalillo County Medical Center just after midnight on July 2, 1996, she had just been born. The sky was thick with butterflies in the few days before she was born. They flew circles around us, alerted us that the birth was near, that this girl they accompanied was about to be born. After she was born in that indigo calm just after midnight I gave her the name, Hokte Tvffolupv, which means Butterfly Girl in Mvskoke.

She was born with the gift of being able to see sharply into the belly of the earth, and with that ability comes the responsibility to speak of what she sees, no matter the difficult truth of it. Her voice is startling in its resonance and depth. She loves the complexity of language and will carry a word in her mouth, tasting it for hours.

The sound of a voice will often reveal a map of destiny. We read these maps unconsciously for intention, to answer unspoken questions, or simply to admire the quality of song in the nuance of inflection. Our voices change according to our response to the intimate emotional landscape, to the shape of our evolving nations.

Her appearance here with us marks a convergence of all of us, yet she is ultimately, definitely, herself: a soul who will say no and mean it despite the will of others, a lover of horses, cats and other creatures, one who has already walked through fire.

The End

◎

(Pol Pot, infamous leader of the Khmer Rouge, responsible for the killing of thousands, died peacefully in his sleep April 1998. His body was burned on a stack of old tires, tended to by a few exhausted soldiers. In the midst of the burning the fist of the corpse saluted.)

The dark was thicker than dark. I was a stranger there. It was a room
of ten thousand strangers, in a city of millions more.

The park across the street was heavy with new leaves
with an unbearable sensual drift.

I had been sleeping for a few hours, and the room was thick with cedar
and root medicine. I wasn't dead though I was traveling

through the dark. The lower gods pounded the pipes for my
attention, the bed swayed with the impact of unseen

energy. No one saw it. No one saw anything
because it was dark and in the middle of the night and it was just

a hotel room, one of millions of hotel rooms all over
the world, filled with strangers looking for refuge,

sleep, for sex or love. We were a blur of distinctions,
made a fragrance like a glut of flowers or piss on concrete.

Every detail mattered
utterly, especially in the dark, when I began traveling.

And I was alone though the myth of the lonely stranger is a lie
by those who think they own everything, even the earth

and the entrails and breath of the earth. This was the end.
It was Cambodia or some place like it, and the sun

was coming up, barely over the green in the restless shiver of
a million singing birds. Humans were wrapping

a body for burial. It stank of formaldehyde. It was a failed clay
thing, disheveled and ordinary. They rolled it

into a box and dragged it to a stack of trash. Why have I come here
I asked the dark, whose voice is the roar of history as it travels

with the thoughts of humans who have made the monster.
The fire was lit

fed with a wicker chair, a walking cane and several busted
tires to make it hot. What I had

feared in the dark was betrayal, so I found myself there
in the power of wreckage. There was no pause

in the fighting. The killer's charred fist pointed toward the sky,
gave an order though no one heard it

for the crackle and groan of grease. The fire was dark
in its brightness and could be seen by anyone

on the journey, the black smoke a dragon in the sky.
This was not the end.

I was attracted by a city, by a park heavy with new leaves,
by a particular flower burning in the dark.

I was not a stranger there.

compassionate fire

Everything was ending the night I found myself at the Gramercy Park Hotel in New York City, though it was spring and the air was urgent with the perfume of fresh leaves and new flowers. I was restless that night as I tried to sleep in the hotel room, accompanied by the sounds of the thousands who surrounded me in that city, souls clammering in the present, from the past and present and possible future. I had left a nine-year relationship and though I had flourished with the end my next move was tentative. The newspaper that morning had included a graphic story of the death and anticlimactic burial of Pol Pot, infamous leader of the Khmer Rouge. How ironic that a man responsible for the cruel deaths of thousands would die peacefully in the jungle on a cheap flowered mattress. He was surrounded by tired guards, who later cremated the body on a stack of tires, junk, and a few belongings. Rumors are that he may have been poisoned. Even so, he was to go gently in his sleep, unlike the thousands he violently murdered.

Perhaps there is a current called "the end" and we catch the wave of it by luck, karma or some other means of logic. Each process has a cycle. *The end* is one part of the cycle and it recurs according to the spin. That night *the end* slithered through the unconsciousness of the city. It appeared in the dark vaguely as a giant lizard, close to the Mvskoke descriptions of a tie snake, a monster from the waters of the deep conscious. It whipped around, knocking dreamers into nightmares, dragging us through our fears at the deepest point of the night.

Not far from dawn my spirit jumped up, out of my body and began traveling through history. This is not unusual. The need for this particular trip was especially urgent. I needed to see my way through the end, to know the utter end of a relationship, for example, or to see the utter end of evil. I felt susceptible to danger. The journey is difficult and you may find yourself in a field of cremation fires, caught in the keening of grief. You will make it to the other side though it may be be an eternity in human time, a blink in star time.

This world is layered with flowers and birds to make it lighter. I smelled roses in my room, the sticky ash of human fire, the ozone of spirits. I stood there at that fire as evil burned. The land was rich with the songs of birds who had kept singing through all the killings, through the slash of torture, the burn of betrayal.

Why does evil exist? I ask the question we all continue to ask. And why does evil often sit in the chairs of rulers, presiding over history, over human and other lives they are charged to protect? We are the ones who give these people power. Andrew Jackson was made president after being medaled with high war honors by the U.S. Government for killing Mvskoke women and children who were resisting being forced from their homelands.

In this age leaders seem to be chosen according to the ability to acquire power and money, not because of their outstanding gifts of service, compassion and love for the community.

Destruction is part of any process like weeding, and we need to constantly hone ourselves to be made strong, not to rule and destroy but to continue toward a beautiful sense of meaning and order. There is an exact address of compassion and in this place even Pol Pot and Andrew Jackson will one day open their eyes. But it is sometimes difficult to translate this knowing into the here and now where men like Pol Pot and Andrew Jackson are honored for their acts and are perceived as powerful and women raising children are not.

Once I traveled years through the dark and found myself in India at a funeral pyre of a teacher whom I loved compassionately, fiercely. He sat up though the fire raged around him. He was cool and composed and though the fire appeared to consume him it didn't touch him. He turned to smile at me, transformed me with his embodiment of perfect peace.

And then like most humans I walked back into the world I had made. Back to my quick impatience at any small thing. What a small memory! And I have to laugh at myself, and keep going through the end.

Emergence

It's midsummer night. The light is skinny;
a thin skirt of desire skims the earth.
Dogs bark at the musk of other dogs
and the urge to go wild.
I am lingering at the edge
of a broken heart, striking relentlessly
against the flint of hard will.
It's coming apart.
And everyone knows it.
So do squash erupting in flowers
the color of the sun.
So does the momentum of grace
gathering allies
in the partying mob.
The heart knows everything.
I remember when there was no urge
to cut the land or each other into pieces,
when we knew how to think
in beautiful.
There is no world like the one surfacing.
I can smell it as I pace in my square room,
the neighbor's television
entering my house by waves of sound.
Makes me think about buying
a new car, another kind of cigarette
when I don't need another car
and I don't smoke cigarettes.
A human mind is small when thinking
of small things.
It is large when embracing the maker
of walking, thinking and flying.
If I can locate the sense beyond desire,

I will not eat or drink
until I stagger into the earth
with grief.
I will locate the point of dawning
and awaken
with the longest day in the world.

the crow and the snake

◎

The backyard patio had become the oasis for the neighborhood birds. The crows, starlings, sparrows and pigeons met there early every morning for gossip, their morning baths, and their first meal of the day, attracted by the dog's food and water supplies. As with all creatures, some left refreshed and got on immediately with the business of the day, while others couldn't get enough dog chow or gossip as they lazed around all afternoon, hopping around the patient and lonely dog who didn't seem to mind the noisy gathering or sharing his food and water.

One day the very busy humans who lived there thought things had gone too far. The dog's fresh water had become the bathing system for hundreds of birds, and though the birds ate relatively little they scattered dog food all over the patio and made a terrible clutter. The humans were tired of cleaning up bird mess and the clatter of gossip broke their sleep and set their teeth on edge. So they had a meeting to figure out what to do.

Snakes were one of the most feared enemies of the birds and they were few and far between in this city. Cats were the most common enemy, one they battled daily, but no cat would venture into the dog's territory. He was a huge dog and his greatest weakness was chasing cats. He would break off a leash, leap over the wall at the sight of a cat. It was a compulsion with him, though he never got close enough to catch one. He convinced himself it was the chase that really mattered. It was deeply satisfying like nothing else. So as the birds talked, lazed and bathed he dreamed about chasing cats.

The humans decided to buy a huge rubber snake to frighten the birds. They weren't sure it would work but they were willing to try anything. That night they curled the snake into an alert circle next to the food and water supplies. The next morning they awoke to the alarmed cries of the birds, who were disturbed at the presence of this predator next to their favorite hangout. The birds cried, "snake" in their various languages and gathered in the largest tree high above the house, above the patio, dog and humans and now the invader snake, which had ruined their prized meeting place. They discussed the situation for several hours, sent scouts down to see if they could find out anything about the kind of snake it was, where it came from, its intentions and its plans for leaving. The snake was silent, stealthy and so controlled it could appear dead. These were the most dangerous.

Now the birds would have to go back to their old routine in which they raided dog and cat dishes in scavenger groups of two and three birds all over the neighborhood. It was a tricky business to run the gauntlet of cats, and humans, particularly the young human males. In this house they were protected by the dog, who had actually learned their names and inquired after their families. And the humans had been tolerant in the beginning.

The dog didn't fear snakes; he didn't see any reason for alarm. The snake didn't bother him, nor was he too friendly. He came to miss his bird friends, who, though they were often a nuisance, even standing on his back and wakening him while he was in the midst of a particular delicious dream chase, were his friends. The humans were glad that the snake trick had worked but had to admit they missed some of the storytelling of the birds, particularly that of the crows, whose language was closer to human languages.

For a long time the birds stayed away, though sometimes they would fly by the patio, nostalgic for the good times, the stories that seemed to naturally arise after a good meal, a good bath.

The oldest crow, who happened to be the wisest (and this isn't always the case), had this gut feeling that something was strange about this snake who suddenly appeared on the patio. He was like the others who when they saw the snake were guided by the primordial knot in the brain that said, "run." There was no thinking involved, instinct took over the muscles, brain and heart.

He too like the others would reminisce about the good times. That was the place he had met his favorite wife, a beautiful shiny one who had a gift for finding prized bits of food. She always gave him the best pieces and they had great times together the few years they had and loved watching the sunrise together. She was killed by a cat who stalked her while she scavanged the trash cans in the alley. He never paired with anyone else after that, preferred to contemplate the deeper meaning of life and picked the scab of his sorrow as he lived at the edge of his crow community.

He knew this wasn't all there was, this struggle for food, territory, and survival in a city that kept churning up more trash. Dreams came to him and gave insight into the history of crows and possibilities for their evolving place in this world. The respect for his knowledge grew in the birds' world, even as he contemplated the appearance of the snake, an event that destroyed a happy rhythm in their lives.

No one thought to further question the identity of the snake, to understand why the snake did not move and kept silent vigil at the water and food oasis. The old crow decided to solve the mystery. He knew he would die soon and he was too wise to fear death. If it be by snake, so be it.

Without the knowledge of the others the crow began to keep vigil and stood on a chair in the patio watching this snake. The humans saw him, perceived him thinking, measuring and weighing the curled snake. Even they were impressed by the wisdom in his eyes, the careful way he observed and pondered the monster that had changed his world.

He walked around the snake, then touched the dreaded enemy and stepped back, blinking his eyes as he waited for the strike. He touched the cold snake again. Nothing! He then kicked at the snake. Again, nothing! This snake was not alive, never had been; they'd been fooled by the humans. Before traveling to call a meeting to tell the others he stopped for a bite to eat, a bath and a visit with the dog, who greeted him warmly.

The bird meeting went long into the night and ended with a bitter disagreement and a separation between those who thought the crow was lying, because they had seen the snake themselves and they were going to believe what they saw, and those who believed the wisdom of the crow and prepared to return to their beloved meeting place. Those who thought the crow was lying wished to protect their friends they thought were foolish for wishing to believe what they considered a lie. When they could not garner agreement they turned and walked away and were never seen again by those who believed.

The next morning a few birds were gathered at the meeting place though they were raw with the hurt of the separation. They bathed, ate of the plentiful dog food nuggets and recounted the history of the place and discussed what they had learned.

The humans saw that the crow had discovered the secret of the snake and took it back into the house. They often looked for the wise crow and would catch a glimpse of him once in a while, then there came a time they never saw him again.

And it was never quite the same in that neighborhood for the crows, pigeons, starlings and sparrows, or the humans and the dog, who missed his old crow friend. But there were new creatures born: human, dog and bird, and they were always told the story of the birds and the snake.

Songs from the House of Death, Or How to Make It Through to the End of a Relationship

◎

for Donald Hall

1.

From the house of death there is rain.
From rain is flood and flowers.
And flowers emerge through the ruins
of those who left behind
stores of corn and dishes,
turquoise and bruises
from the passion
of fierce love.

2.

I run my tongue over the skeleton
jutting from my jaw. I taste
the grit of heartbreak.

3.

The procession of spirits
who walk out of their bodies
is ongoing. Just as the procession
of those who have loved us
will go about their business
of making a new house
with someone else who smells
like the dust of a strange country.

4.

The weight of rain is unbearable to the sky
eventually. Just as desire will
burn a hole through the sky
and fall to earth.

5.

I was surprised by the sweet embrace
of the perfume of desert flowers after the rain
though after all these seasons
I shouldn't be surprised.

6.

All cities will be built and then destroyed.
We built too near the house of the gods of lightning,
too close to the edge of a century.
What could I expect,
my bittersweet.

7.

Even death who is the chief of everything
on this earth (all undertakings, all matters of human
form) will wash his hands, stop to rest under
the cottonwood before taking you from me
on the back of his horse.

8.

Nothing I can sing
will bring you back.
Not the songs of a hundred horses running
until they become wind
Not the personal song of the rain
who makes love to the earth.

9.

I will never forget you. Your nakedness
haunts me in the dawn when I cannot distinguish your
flushed brown skin from the burning horizon, or my hands.
The smell of chaos lingers in the clothes
you left behind. I hold you
there.

there is no such thing as a one-way land bridge

◎

I imagine someone walking through the ruins of my house, years later when I am gone and anyone who knew me and my family and nation is gone and there are only stories as to what happened to us. Did we flee from an enemy, or die of famine or floods?

The story depends on who is telling it. A colonizer will say that the people disappeared, though their descendents are still living in the same area and they are going to school with their children. The descendents of the Anasazi are my granddaughters and will be their children and yet they are catalogued as "disappeared." If it can be postulated that a people came to a natural end, that no one was there, the land was abandoned, then the colonizer will assume a right of ownership.

For years, predominant anthropological theory of the study of North American Indians was and still is the Bering Strait theory, that is, that North America was settled by a relatively late migration of peoples from Asia. This translated that prior rights of occupation was tentative, and made land claims of the indigenous peoples hold less weight, for if we were recent immigrants, too, then who are we to make claims?

The Bering Strait theory assumes that a land bridge was marked one way. The logic of that notion is so faulty as to be preposterous. There is no such thing as a one-way land bridge. People, creatures and other life will naturally travel back and forth. Just as we will naturally intermarry, travel up and down rivers, cross oceans, fly from Los Angeles to Oklahoma for a powwow.

The fault of that theory and so many others in the western world is that Indians are somehow less than human, or at least not as advanced as western European cultured humans. We are constantly being defined from the point of view of the colonizer. We are human and live complex and meaningful lives. I like the response given to an anthropologist when he asked a teacher in a particular Asian culture about ideology and theory. "What ideology? We just dance."

When I am home in Oklahoma at the stomp grounds we may talk about the complexities of meaning, but to comprehend it, to know it intimately, the intricate context of history and family, is to dance it, to be it.

I think back to the ruins of a house in Chaco Canyon, Anasazi ruins near Crownpoint, New Mexico. The winds are cool and steady and through the years they have eroded the adobe. There is no protection from the sun and rain. Tourists quickly pass through ruins. The clouds, too, walk on. Everything keeps moving. Even me, moved by my thoughts through the house, through time. I converse with my own death, which will one day leave a track behind me, like the ruins of this house.

There was a woman here who was loved. She was good to look at because she was a quick and imaginative thinker. She liked the view of the peach orchard from the southern window, and loved the turquoise earrings that her mother had given her at her marriage. Her life mattered, utterly, to herself, to her children, to those she loved, to the birds she scattered crumbs to after the family had eaten. This was her house, and years later the house still remembered her, though it was almost gone and the woman's spirit had flown to the other side.

Forgetting

It will be easy enough to forget how to breathe.
It's an acquired skill, fueled by the animal need
to stand up and gather together in the world
to hunt through chaos for a sliver of meat.
It's darker this morning than
the last, and when I breathe this sharp air
I sense the shape and intent of the field of hurt
and it's larger than this earth. I've stood
at the Bay of Bengal looking toward the end.
It's past the last wave.
I don't want to talk to anyone about the raw shiver
of nerves as I pace back and forth
over the rotten territory of all the bad things
that have ever been done, beginning
with the first thief to cross over
into the nation of the heart.
If I peer from the top of this canyon and look out
over the Pacific I see myself standing at the edge
in the sand as the stranger in cowboy boots
among a crowd of saris and sandals
in the field of ancient miracles.
I had never been so far away then
I am even farther away this morning
disappearing into the mirror of sadness.
All the poems in the world leap
to the reason for the first breath.
I was attracted like everyone else to jump
into humanness, choking on blood and water,
lungs flapping like a fish dangling in air.
I return to the baby
kicking in the bassinet
to that little heart in the shape of a star

breaking open.
I return to the origin of wind and how
it depends on water and how the ocean
is an insurmountable deep
I imagine someone else's life: watching
television with a lover, a bag of popcorn
and the magnificence of skin between them.
They aren't thinking about anything at all.
A delicious nothing.
And I am marooned without the blessing
of water, still fighting to see over the edge
to the water gods who are powerful.
They are larger than the earth. And the gulf
of sadness to them is nothing
but a temporary ditch to be filled up.
Forget history and how it has a way
of looping until you slap up against the chest
of an enemy who desires you and hates himself
for loving himself in you.
I'd rather be naked and flushed with the afterburn of love.
But what is sorrowful is cheap
and easy to obtain—this by the same exact law that maintains
weeds grow in battalions with no bidding
while humans and corn
need constant reassurance
of songs.
Now I worry about how any of us are going to make it
through the bloodstream to the ceremony
for returning from the enemy.
So I change directions with the assistance of a metal bird,
climb through cloud mountains and over blue spirit rivers—
I've been here before, packing it all up after selling everything

and traveling until I become a stranger again
in a sea of strangers.
A human can be larger than life
diminished to a wisp of smoke on the horizon
and then a gull distracts you
with an argument over fish,
and everyone's gone.
Some things I will never forget.

sleepwalkers

In this life I have lived many different lives. The first was as an infant and young girl in the early fifties. It was as if I had fallen through a hole in the sky to a postwar house in Tulsa, Oklahoma. Sometimes I knew I was still falling and the journey didn't always make sense. My life revolved around a father and mother, two brothers and sister, segregation of people and ideas and in a city that depressed me with intimate human cruelties, then astounded me with the sheer beauty of sunlight on dew.

Consciousness is larger than what most people accepted as reality. I didn't know any better, I hadn't gone to school yet, so I traveled freely through layers past the physical world. When everyone else slept my spirit excited to exit my body, and I traveled up and down the neighborhood, first walking through fences to play with the neighborhood dogs, then flying to the moon and other planets, through time and space to other dramas. It was normal. And what I learned kept me sane in the small world I was living in. And then I went to school.

Immense memory stored in the minds of the sun and planets was lost in the translation to kindergarten. Soon I forgot my journeys and how to travel because in this system of thinking and being it wasn't possible to separate from the body and fly. You needed metal and engineering for such a feat. That was one of the first things I learned. Another was the propensity of humans to allow others to think for them.

Once in kindergarten we were coloring on huge sheets of newsprint. I loved the smell of the paper and crayons and could reverie on pure smell alone, disappear into a meditative groove as I created. I loved art, and remember coloring a circle of people, all joined together, a design of sorts. I always filled in the skin with orange. I knew I was not white (though I am light-skinned) nor was I full-blooded Indian, but nonetheless I was aware of the difference. I looked up when I was finished and was shocked by the similarity of all the other children's drawings. They were drawing and copying virtually the same house, square with a chimney and square windows, the same lollipop trees, the same sun and birds.

I asked, because I really wanted to know, "why are you copying each other?" They then looked at my drawing and began copying me. That the other children would choose to copy rather than create for themselves bothered me for days but how would I begin to find the words to discuss such an observation?

In first grade I caused a major uproar because I dared to color a ghost green on our thermofaxed Halloween coloring sheets. I knew there were green ghosts because I had seen them. But the children crowded around my desk didn't accept my vision and demanded to know why my ghost wasn't white. They were utterly threatened by my departure from the agreed-upon truth, that ghosts were white. They couldn't accept my green-ghost theory. This kind of thinking had already closed down the classroom.

Each of my many lives, from teenage mother to tribal-jazz-rock musician, is marked by similar incidents, and a frustration of being unable to translate what it is I bring back from my travels. This dogmatic system of conformity proscribes the shape of thought, of everything in this Puritan-influenced country (especially the Bible Belt), from being forced to wear dresses to school for girls (I broke this in the fourth grade by begging for and getting the same school clothes as my brother, jeans and shirts. I was finally comfortable) to believing there was only one road to God in a world of many roads.

Forgetting is so easy in this illusion and I understand the need to sleepwalk. The field of hurt is immense and to venture outside the lines can be tricky and difficult. It's too much to bear sometimes. But the complexity of the mind behind the larger system of knowledge is stunning and will break through any way it can, and is most likely to do so through the words or the images of a child, or any other artist.

The Path to the Milky Way Leads Through Los Angeles

There are strangers above me, below me and all around me and we are all
strange in this place of recent invention.
This city named for angels appears naked and stripped of anything resembling
the shaking of turtle shells, the songs of human voices on a summer night
outside Okmulgee.
Yet, it's perpetually summer here, and beautiful. The shimmer of gods is easier
to perceive at sunrise or dusk,
when those who remember us here in the illusion of the marketplace
turn toward the changing of the sun and say our names.
We matter to somebody,
We must matter to the strange god who imagines us as we revolve together in
the dark sky on the path to the Milky Way.
We can't easily see that starry road from the perspective of the crossing of
boulevards, can't hear it in the whine of civilization or taste the minerals of
planets in hamburgers.
But we can buy a map here of the stars' homes, dial a tone for dangerous love,
choose from several brands of water or a hiss of oxygen for gentle rejuvenation.
Everyone knows you can't buy love but you can still sell your soul for less
        than a song to a stranger who will sell it to someone else for a profit
until you're owned by a company of strangers
in the city of the strange and getting stranger.
I'd rather understand how to sing from a crow
who was never good at singing or much of anything
but finding gold in the trash of humans.
So what are we doing here I ask the crow parading on the ledge of falling that
hangs over this precarious city?
Crow just laughs and says *wait, wait and see* and I am waiting and not seeing
anything, not just yet.
But like crow I collect the shine of anything beautiful I can find.

the power of never

Never is the most powerful word in the English language, or perhaps any language. It's magic. Everytime I have made an emphatic pronouncement invoking the word *never*, whatever follows that I don't want to happen happens. Never has made a fool of me many times. The first time I remember noticing the powerful effect of this word I was a student at Indian school. My best friend, Belinda Gonzalez, and I were filling out our schedules for spring semester. She was Blackfeet, a voice major from Yakima, Washington. I was a painting major and checking out times for painting and drawing courses. She suggested I sign up for drama class with her. I said no, I will never get on a stage. Despite my initial protest I did sign up for drama class and soon was performing in one of the first all-native drama and dance troupes in the country, and now I make my living performing. Never is that powerful!

And it doesn't matter when the statement is made, never makes its cruel spin as it hunts down a dreaded fate. It must be quite attractive in the epistemological world, a being with dark, luminous eyes, the physique of a cat. You will get on a stage, or in this case, you will move to Los Angeles at some point on your journey because you have just foolishly stated to a circle of friends that Los Angeles is the last place in the world you would live, you would never live there because it's smoggy, too much traffic, too many strangers and besides it is going to fall off into the ocean after one too many earthquakes, or one too many stupid movies.

So I moved to Los Angeles, into the heart of the beast, just off Hollywood and Wilcox to an apartment complex harboring a myriad of fools like me, some who probably made the same statement regarding the possibility of moving to Los Angeles, using that same word, never. Needless to say I was in shock as a new arrivee, from a quiet adobe condo near a bird sanctuary in Albuquerque where the daily music of life was the song of the sun moving across the sky, doves swinging on the telephone wires and other birds who considered the Rio Grande river valley a spa for their personal renewal.

I spoke with the crows before leaving for Los Angeles. They were the resident storytellers whose strident and insistent voices added the necessary dissonance for color. They had cousins in California, and gave me names and addresses, told me to look them up. They warned me too what they had heard about attitude there. And they were right. Attitude was thick, hung from the would-be's and has-beens and think-they-ares, so thick that I figured it was the major source of the smog.

And then there were the beautiful days when the perfume of flowers was everything and there appeared to be nothing else in the world, not the violence, the winos breaking bottles in the alley, the Spice Girls going up Hollywood Boulevard on a double-decker bus with low-flying helicopters accompanying them. The crows' cousins kept me company in that sometimes lonely and strange place as they paced the ledges of the crumbling buildings in my neighborhood.

One of the crows lived two apartments down from me. We lived on the third floor. He introduced himself to me shortly after I moved in when we met one day in the hallway. He gallantly took off his silk hat and bowed, said, "my name is R——, we take care of each other here." His slick black hair was perfectly groomed, his clothes shiny with money. Hip-hop music came through his door, and he had a steady stream of company, a perpetual party. He was always polite though the crowd of buyers grew large and raucous. Last I heard he was evicted for selling drugs, this crow with manners and a taste for the fine things in life.

I've considered using the power of never by trying for the opposite effect. For example: I will never win the lottery, or there will never be peace in this world. It won't work. It never will.

Holdup

for Greg Sarris

We were the twins, given birth to by a mother who loved the talk of gods.
She slept with the sun in the sky to have us—just when this world was ending.

And in that shifting time there was much danger, isn't that when these things tend to
happen? Giants are born and we could be swallowed by the monster.

That day we fled the changing of the worlds, we ran with tender blessings
into the streets, carried sharpened arrows and the promise of a father

who was a stranger. He could have been a musician, or a cowboy
but our mother pointed to the sun, and we burned brightly in our skins.

We went to school, worked jobs at the factory, and learned to buy everything
we needed. We forgot the smell and warning of the monster, and the reason

for the journey. The sun zigzagged across the land to watch us, made
a nimbic web that embraced us. Most humans breathed and died

without knowing they breathed planets. It's easy to get sidetracked and difficult
to see farther than the skin houses we walk this earth in. The perfume of flowers

and we want to be a flower. One night we stared at the glittering dark for clues.
For anything to sing, to shine—convinced someone had forgotten us.

In the whirlpool of the city the monster found us, walking in the glamour
without our arrows. It was two young boys who could have been our brothers,

they held us up, said they would kill us, as if we were no longer human,
or close to eagle. The payoff easy money, an itch for power. The moon

said nothing to them, neither did the creatures matter, or the flowers
who have a heart they share among themselves. We wanted to kill

the monster so they would not destroy the earth and take it with them,
or erase the dreams of humans in the ordinary world.

We gave them all our money in the whirling wake of violence,
the sun gleaming in our eyes made them walk the other way.

They wanted love, like we did, but did not know how to say it.
Humans were created by mistake, someone laughed and we came
crawling out. That was the beginning of the drama, we were hooked then.
What a wild dilemma, how to make it to the stars on a highway slick
with fear. The spirit of the story could smell the danger, climbed down
the clouds because things had gone too far. It breathed in life
from all directions, included the running boys in the beautiful pattern.
We followed.

twins meet up with monsters in the glittering city

◎

It is late on a balmy spring evening in Hollywood and we are headed to our friends June and Michael's to drop off a manuscript and say hello. On the drive over from the gym we talk about our fathers as we often do when we make our way in this city of lost angels. There's a terrible beauty here that few acknowledge; it's in the angle of light. Tonight all the flowers have decided to open at once and we are flooded by memory.

Greg's father, Pomo and Filipino, was legendary in his fury. He was a boxer who felt rudely trapped by the shape of this world. He squared off against it and went to war. He fought behind the shield of a broken heart that he had carried from one life to the next.

My father, a Mvskoke Creek, was a mechanic whose sensual charisma made him attractive to danger. Women fell in love with him and were willing to sacrifice everything to be in his orbit. It was a messy orbit, unpredictable and rough, but the man was a great dancer.

These fathers were linked by the nature of being born Indian in a post-colonial world, and by a love for water. Greg's father ran the bars up and down the Pacific Coast from Laguna Beach to Pomo country. My father lived for communion with water, whether it be one of the many man-made lakes in Oklahoma or later the Gulf Coast next to which he died. Humans are mostly water and we must have it to live, but we can also drown in as little as a fistful of water, a cup the size of a heart.

Greg didn't know his father when he was a boy. He was given up for adoption. His mother was a stunning Jewish girl who defied her family by going out with the dark outlaw who was Greg's father. She had vision beyond her 16 years, a best friend who survived her told Greg years later. She could see human energies and was wise despite her relative youth. She knew before giving birth that her life would be sacrificed to bring her son into the world and she was willing. She still hovers near him, giving him guidance and much-needed protection from enemies.

When Greg finally tracked down his father he discovered his father had died just a few months before. Death however does not end a journey and Greg will always look for his father even though his father lives in his muscles, his smile, his urge to live by water.

My father was with us until I was eight. He tried to provide a home, make a family with my mother, a striking Cherokee-mixed woman he met while out dancing. I could say that the loss of his mother when he was an infant, the brutality of his father and the confusion of being Indian in a society in which his existence was shameful were too much for this man whose nerve endings dangled far outside his elegant, long body, and he left us, but who ever knows the how and why of a journey, or the reason behind the particulars? Others have lost their mothers, like Greg, others grow up Indian in a world in which they were never meant to survive, others have been beaten by their fathers and don't beat their children. What is it in the equation that makes a difference between leaving and staying, surviving or not?

Greg and I further mused we must have had the same stepfather, a man who could love no one, not even our mothers, whom they professed to love, without destroying everything they touched. His stepfather never accepted him, which is perhaps the ultimate abuse. There are stories he harbors in the corners of his heart that he won't even tell me, this friend who tells me everything, including the gory details of romantic liaisons I don't want to know! I've seen the shadow of the monster, seen it try to pin him down, sensed the wrench of grief. I know it in myself.

Our fathers and many of the men of our indigenous nations destroyed themselves with a whirling bright power that was meant to bring new visions to the people. It is still here among us, made strong with every kind act, with the very act of our beautiful survival. Perhaps even the spirits of our fathers have fed this power because their sacrifice showed us the way.

When we get out of the truck we are overwhelmed by the perfume of flowers carried by a breeze tenderly from the Pacific. I am always reminded of the legacy of my father here and his love for water. Though his love for me was flawed he loved me nonetheless and it was while we were together near water we were happiest.

I follow my friend Greg from the truck up the sidewalk to our friends' corner house. I can smell the water of the Pacific in the air. Two young boys approach on the sidewalk. Unconsciously I hang back. Though Greg is big, has the physique of a bodybuilder, and I am discretely muscled from working out, I am still dressed in the body of a woman and am suspicious of any male on the sidewalk day or night. I dislike this state of affairs in the culture. It makes a war zone out of ordinary living.

I hear Greg greet the boys with familiar words, as one would speak to young relatives on the road. Next I hear: "I am going to kill you." I step backwards off the curb into slow motion. A tree rustling with empathy blocks my view of Greg and the boys. I can't see and it feels as if I am dreaming this, until a gun is held to my head by the second boy and he tells me to give him everything. Now they are no longer boys. They are harbingers of death, holding our lives in their childish, dangerous hands.

I am furious and imagine a karate kick, the gun flying up as the boy sprawls disabled on the ground and I turn to take on his partner, but I also know in my lizard brain that this could trigger a panic that could kill my friend and/or myself. And I am aware that I have not heard anything from Greg since the threat and he could be killed any moment, which has now become an eternity of small moments destroying themselves against the perfumed dark.

I split into several tracks of awareness. I can hear the spin of the earth, literally. The urge to live surges through the trees, each blade of grass, each particular flower and leaf surrounding the house of our friends, who are inside getting their children ready for bed and they know nothing of this terrible drama going on next to the white-painted fence.

My death is a huge thing too large to argue with but I do comment that it is a little earlier than we agreed upon. And death says nothing but nods its head. Also, I note to death, I do not want to die without honor, here on the streets of this city by the hands of children, with my friend. I laugh to think of the write-up in the paper: *two prominent Indian writers killed in hold-up in Los Angeles.* It would make a good story, and our enemies would be thrilled.

I think of the twin monster slayer stories I have heard from my Navajo friends. Perhaps the monsters are disguised as these two thieves. Or maybe in their eyes we are the monsters, the ones who appear to have money because of the neighborhood they found us in, our light-skin. I think of my babies but I have to turn my heart the other way or I will dissolve into grief. Yet I know this is not the natural end of this story, not the way our linked destiny had it in mind, and still I know that everything can turn, unnaturally and sudden.

The boy almost shoots me with his cheap gun because he is too uptight to easily pull off my watch. I nervously yank the watch off and give it to him. I give him my wallet with twenty dollars in it, and the beautiful turquoise bracelet I bought for protection. Maybe it is protecting me. I am not dead yet. Strange to find a child in the face of a monster and I want to ask him, "Where is your father?"

Then the boy backs up, his gun pointed at my heart. I can hear Greg's voice in the dark, and see the boys backing off, their guns aimed at us to keep us from bringing the police. They turn to walk off into the twisted maw of the glittering city, counting our money, our possessions as bounty. Only then do I hear the pounding of my heart. Only then do I feel the tremble of Greg's life as we hold each other up.

Part II

Returning from

the Enemy

Preparations

You are showering in the artificial light of the motel room
    before dawn when most earthly spirits
are returning from the dreaming. Your familiar perfume
    is gathered during the night like pollen
from the flowering after a hard male rain.
    Everything is holy in this hour, though holiness
isn't easily perceived in a city of enemies.
    As you turn to dress for war your spirit is accompanied by an antelope
grazing at the edge of fire. The accouterments of battle
    weigh heavily against your thigh. There's a room somewhere
with corn soup and fresh bread, someone who loves you setting the table.
    Humans are the strangest of animals because they make laws
from lies, then reinforce them. We should be like the antelope
    who gratefully drink the rain,
love the earth for what it is—their book of law, their heart.

ceremony

When considering ceremony the act of preparation is most crucial. Each day is a ceremonial progression in which every human takes part. We do so either consciously or unconsciously. You can prepare by setting the alarm clock and jumping into the world with anxiety, or you can still set the alarm clock, but take time to prepare for the day, by singing, by prayer, by a small acknowledgment of the gift of the day itself.

It has a spirit, this creature called day, and will go on without us, dragging us behind it. Or, we can take part in the ceremony and walk (or run!) with grace into the momentum. For the Mayan this is a science, this naming of the spirits of each day, and by knowing the characteristics of the spirit of each day one can understand the manner in which events will unfold. There's an overall pattern in this calendar that can be examined and if we follow its logical trail we will arrive at the end of the spiral in the memory field of the Milky Way. All this meaning, we can walk or run blindly through the ceremony of our life, a tricky obstacle course no matter the cultural reference points, or incorporate knowledge that will give this journey a heightened sense of meaning, of beauty, despite the terrible complexities and apparent injustices.

Some days we are innately in harmony. We were born to a spirit on a particular day and it jives with the one we are in. Other days are doomed to give us a rough ride and the only way through it is to hang on and get back on again if you get bucked off. Any conscious preparation will allow us to act with steady grace, no matter the fluid destiny.

When I was a child some days were a hiding place for monsters and for events I was not supposed to see. Once a ghost sat on my chest and refused to move. It flew away at dawn because it could not thrive in the truth of harsh sunlight. Shortly thereafter I came down with pneumonia. Once my father sneaked into my room (it also belonged to my sister and two brothers) on the spare cot with a girlfriend. They awakened me with their talk, their lit cigarettes branding the dark. This was another kind of monster that would not leave until daybreak.

It too left sickness as I worried for the condition of love in our house. I could not say what I knew but understood it would break our house. And I felt ashamed that I knew something I could not tell my mother.

After these long nights involving ghosts, or the betrayal of the father, I would get up and go out into the dawn. I would let the sun touch me, clean me, prepare me for the day. It was always astounding to me that the sun could be so intimate though it was light-years away from Tulsa. I could see the energy as it sparkled, fed the plants, entered and left my spirit refreshed. The other creatures, too, made this preparation and they would make all manner of acknowledgment in songs to the maker of the day.

Other spirits were as sweet as honeysuckle and brought happiness and a general ease, like the days that ended with watermelon and a circle of friends with which to share it. Those were the days when our mother felt inspired to sing as she wiped up the messes we made as our trail to the Milky Way led through the kitchen.

Maybe the spirits of the days live in the world above the earth we call dawn and stand reverently as the sun arrives in the appointed place in the east. Flowers, plants, all creatures prepare for the sun's arrival. You can hear the rustle of anticipation as the ultramarine sky turns to a cobalt grey. Deer move towards water to drink. Birds chatter plans for the day. In the distance a few humans begin running towards the east to give the sun encouragement, to make sure the sun returns to bless them.

It's crucial we participate for the sun needs our songs, prayers, acknowledgments. Too often the weight of humans has been carried by others who have not lost their original instructions on how to live with integrity in this system.

The War Zone

Yesterday in the flare of smoke and temper—
we were brilliant warriors weary
from battling each other—
the illuminations of family ghosts
bright red in the storm.

The century is swept toward an inevitable end—
as summer trees sway beneath thunderclouds,
the wind flattening our faces—
Our teeth make refuge for our tongues,
skins pulled tight in the vertigo of fear
under unbearable
pressure.

We go on.

there are as many ways to poetry as there are to God

◎

War is a ritual struggle played out since time immemorial. For North American tribes war wasn't a game for the sport of killing, rather a test for bravery and skill. To touch the enemy without being harmed proved bravery. To walk through a fire of enemy arrows meant that you were standing firm inside your own power with help garnered from the not-so-ordinary world. My name, Harjo, which is an Anglicized version of *Hadjo*, meaning "so brave you're crazy," is a title of war for those who were fearless. It is quite a name to live up to, and why, I say, there are so many Harjos in our tribe, because we are known for our bravery.

Wars used to involve the skills of practitioners of magic, sometimes exclusively. Conjuring skills which included battalions of help from the spiritual realm proved the power of one group over another. In my tribe when there were disagreements between tribes, a final decision was sometimes reached through the challenge of a stickball game, a game that was often a ferocious fight that usually included both men and women. This decision was respected. There was no need for pen and paper.

Humans seem to need a way to express ritualized aggression, to test the limits of the body and mind against another, ultimately against oneself. Football is one means. Warfare is another. Competitive sports in general mimic war and the tactics of war. There are many forms and strategies for warfare, some brilliant and compassionate, even, others with no coherent plan, integrity. Bombing a country and sending troops for combat against a nation who is no military threat but has resources you desire appear to characterize contemporary western-style warfare. Here there is no intimate knowledge of the enemy, no reason for the fight other than greed, and, in the end, no integrity.

In most world conflicts in the news both church and business interests have been and continue to be major instigators of war. The church is fueled by a righteous zeal and the need to acquire and control souls, business interests by greed. Multinational corporations destroy the land, and ultimately people and the ways of a people. You can see them setting up business in the wake of violence after they have instigated it. Missionaries and Bible translators work to convert, then attempt to destroy cultures and languages to supplant a system and language as a superior alternative construct.

I don't agree with the need to proselytize and force conversion. Mvskokes who practice a belief system that was given to us at the beginning of time do not feel a need to go out and convert non-Mvskokes to Mvskoke beliefs and rituals. What is the source of this need to devour peoples, cultures, and resources throughout the so-called third world? This is the same force that drove our people out of our lands in what is now known as Georgia and Alabama, followed us to Indian Territory and took our lands there. We still struggle with those same interests in court because they still wish to annihilate us, want us to bow down to their gods of commerce and time.

There are many roads to knowledge in this world. I reminded a student once who tried to force his narrow religious opinion on me and the class that there are as many ways to God as there are to poetry.

War is an ultimate test of character. It's not a route that most of us choose, but many of us wind up there, as a warrior protecting our land and people or as a child on the battlefield with gun in hand. You have to make the best of it and travel with grace through hell. When you are placed on the firing line do you kill and rape women, children and the defenseless? How do you maintain integrity? Why are you fighting? Is it for defense? What do you do with this new knowledge of human cruelty that is inevitably born of warfare?

A young Anishnabe man was sent to Vietnam. He wanted to go fight for his country.* There is honor in this, to defend the land and your people, though

*The United States is a conglomeration of indigenous tribal nations existing within an imposed federal government. This is a major paradox, but it is a reality.

obviously this particular war evokes many questions as to such defense, such necessity. He lasted through two tours of duty without being killed, though as an Indian man he was called on to walk point, head the most dangerous reconnaissance missions. When he landed on the West Coast after leaving the world of fire and ash he could not stop fighting He fought his way from one city in Indian country to another, one bar to another; he could not stop. One morning he awakened in a field of corn in the middle of the prairie, weary with the struggle of the fight that had not ended when he left Vietnam. It had rooted itself in him and he had to admit he could not control it and worst of all could not make sense of the huge monster of violence that had devoured him and others who looked like him.

A spirit found him there that spring morning and was the first to talk to him about what was happening inside him. Told him that he was addicted to violence, explained that as a young man when his tender field of human energy was in the state of becoming he was thrown into a vortex of violence. He was not prepared. He became addicted to the high of danger. Now he had to let this violent whirlwind go and the spirit would help him, and the spirit did.

The Whirlwind

Faster and faster
she whirls in the dark, the jealous
green dark, the make-witchcraft-
in-the-holes dark. Faster and faster.
Here is a hole made by a cigarette.
I couldn't stop it then, she said,
and I won't stop it now.
Faster and faster.
I want that lover of sweet madness,
that powwow prancer
I want prettier than you,
faster and faster.
That car, that house,
that child on your hip,
a cigarette,
faster and faster she whirls
up trash,
the shack she put her mother in,
the man she put a contract on,
the baby in the mirror,
faster and faster.
I can't stop now, she said, *see how*
beautiful I am. I am brighter than you
in my green clothes of power. I am
breakneck and dancer. I am
faster and faster.
And the smoke from the cigarette
laced with curses and envy,
makes a thousand holes in the dark,
the whiplash chasm going
faster and faster.
Let the smoke find its way,

she cries, *faster and faster.*
To the heart of disaster
the smug thief of my dreams.
Faster and faster she blows the smoke
meant for danger, for killing and
maiming, for stealing of power.
She tries to enter my breathing,
and then the gates
of believing,
to the place of let go.
Faster and faster, the thing urges her
on. This thing made of acid
of heartbreak and hatred.
It feeds on itself, decay
and disaster.
I can't find a way, she cries
go faster and faster.

Through the age of monsters
through childhood terror
through forced migrations
and starvation of relatives
then the drum of the heart beating
faster and faster.

To the truth of the matter
it is turned back.
To the source of all jealousy
it turns back.
To the childhood abuser
it is turning back.
To the hole of *if only*

it is back.
To a moth diving, its wings
on fire back
To the heart of compassion
To the place before
and after
you.

all your enemies will be vanquished

◎

While I was in Madras, India, for a collaboration with Anita Ratnam, a South Indian dancer, and her musicians, I visited a Vedic astrologer. I have a great respect for this complex science involving mathematical computations, philosophy, knowledge of astronomy and understanding of esoteric texts. It is a very exact science in the hands of a professional practitioner and has proved itself for centuries.

Forming the basis of this science is the understanding that we are all heavenly bodies in a dynamic interchange with the earth, sun, other planets and virtually all life. Planets do have energy and speak to each other and interact with humans. The energy of planets can be measured and there are literally exchanges of energy between them, a conversation if you will, an exchange of consciousness. We are a community together, breathe together.

When Europeans first observed my people and the respect we had for the sun they interpreted our reverence as sun worship. It wasn't sun worship, rather a respect for a gifted being who decided to stay here and take care of us, though it had other possibilities for its life.

The place and time of our first breath, our agreement to be here, set the tone for the rest of the journey. There is a shape to this agreement based on a configuration of planetary energies and the place we stand on the earth, and we begin a relationship that intimately involves this time and place. The ripple of the path is shaped by that vulnerable and powerful moment of becoming human. It can be mapped.

The astrologer and I discussed his predictions for my life. Most concurred with what I already knew to be true within my sense of knowing at that given moment. *Knowing* is a fluid process, though some events are deeply rooted and practically fixed. The most enigmatic statement was, "By 19— all of your enemies will be vanquished."

That was a rather outrageous statement, I thought, though I relished the notion and we discussed it for over an hour at least, both of us reaching to understand the other's unfamiliar accent over tea and incense. There is energetic basis for such a statement though the logic doesn't translate into western determinism—it slips easier into a Mvskoke shape of possibility.

Certain enemies who I wouldn't mind vanquished came to mind immediately, including a man who continues to try and turn my son against me, a woman who waged a campaign to discredit me, others who attack me, as well as my old friend, fear.

Yesterday as the trade winds tattooed the house, turned the mango tree into a green wave and I worked on business plans, I remembered the astrologer and his confident statement on the destiny of my enemies. It's about time, I thought, as I fumed impatiently over yet some other detail in the events of the day.

Fear is the potent elixir that motivates enemies. And there can be no enemies when there is no fear. Fear makes an illusion of separation.

Once I was being attacked by a monster in the dream world. It seethed pure evil and each breath sucked out precious oxygen. The monster lumbered toward me to destroy me. I was utterly terrified but there was no place to run. The room was small and getting smaller. I felt the rattle of phlegm as the thing's fire breath touched my neck. I was exhausted. Then I woke up inside the dream and flew to the ceiling to escape, but the reach of this monster was extraordinary. Then as if I were a balloon fear rapidly left me through an opening in my feet. I stood and faced the monster who then tried to touch me. His hand went through me because there was no fear to keep it there. Then he was gone.

Returning from the Enemy

for my father

◎

1.

It's time to begin. I know it and have dreaded the knot of memory as it unwinds in my gut.

Behind me the river is steady and laps the jetty. Winds purr through the grass.

The wake of history is a dragline behind me. I am linked to my father, my son, my daughter. We are relatives of deep water.

Even the ghost crab disappearing into white gravel cannot escape the weight. The clacking of his joints makes a staccato against the danger.

Even a friend beside me in this perilous part of the journey stumbles on the slick of knowledge.

And the enemy who pressed guns to our heads to force us to Oklahoma still walks in the mind of the people.

But I hear relatives' voices in the wind as we gather for the reckoning. I carry fire in my hands to the edge of the water.

And continue to believe we will make it through the bloodstream to the ceremony for returning from the enemy.

It's easy to respect our ancestors. They are not fully present here with all their flaws, though some have perfected knowledge and can walk back and forth through the walls of fire and history. They will not save us from ourselves, though they can manuever the pattern and allow meaning to emerge from the dark. When my father remembered he was descended from leaders he was ashamed he had hit his wife, his baby. When I was the baby I did not know my father as a warrior. I knew him as an intimate in whose face I recognized myself.

2.

In the flickering mirror of time all events quiver in layers.

Each tree, each trigger of grass,

each small and large wave of water will reveal the raw story.

We climb and keep climbing, our children

wrapped in smallpox blankets to keep

them warm. Spider shows us how to weave

a sticky pattern from the muddy curses of our enemy

to get us safely to the Milky Way.

We had to leave our homes behind us,

just as we were left behind by progress.

We do not want your version of progress.

There are other versions, says Spider who does not consider making webs

to sell to the highest bidder

but keeps weaving and thinking

and including us in the story.

And so my spirit began traveling in the dark before I learned to walk upon the earth that circles so precisely around the sun. This was part of the ritual of becoming human though many had forgotten the reason for being here, and how we influence the shape of the path with our thinking, our speaking and our songs. I was taken through many worlds so that I would remember that this world was not the largest or the most impressive and that it was often the most difficult because those here were prone to violence and forgetfulness. My father wanted to fly but had stopped trying after he was sent as a child to military school in Ponca City. So I was on my own while he partied up and down the green coast of Tulsa, his wings dragging in the parking lots after closing time.

3.

Vertigo is a terrible mode of travel.

It returns you perpetually to the funnel of terror.

I want it to stop and am furious that fear has found me here,

in the sun where people are laughing, doing ordinary things.

I want to be ordinary, I mean, with no worry that my house will be burned

behind me, that my grandchildren will become the enemy.

Here is the gravel singing under my feet, there are gulls

weaving the sky with horizon, alligators watch from the waters.

I walk with my friend to have lunch on the pier. I panic.

I want to know that I am worthy of all this sky,

the earth, this place to breathe.

I peer out from the house I have constructed from the hole in my heart.

I have returned to the homelands beloved by my people

who were marched to the west

by the authority of a piece of paper.

I keep warm by the fire carried through cruelty.

In mythic stories a child can be born of a liaison between the sun and a woman. And then the child is born and the next day the child is no longer a child but a full-grown human. It all happens that fast. And you think you won't repeat anything you judged them for, but there you are picking your own children up from the babysitter after the bars are closed, the same leather jacket as your father, your own perfume instead of your mother's and you stumble a little as you carry them out to the truck. And there are the same stars and you feel like a giant who can accomplish anything. You are ready to change the world, assume your sovereign rights and stand up against the op-pressor in the morning.

4.

Before speech I took language into the soft parts of my body. This was before I could fully digest meaning. It turned into bones, other hard parts:

I have held before me the god of fear. My heart is my house. A whirlwind is blowing it down.

I have bowed my head to those who would disrespect me. My neck appears to be broken in half by shame. I have lost my country.

I have handed my power over to my enemies. My shoulders bear each act of forgetfulness.

I have abandoned my children to the laws of dictators who called themselves priests, preachers, and the purveyors of law. My feet are scarred from the steps taken in the direction of freedom.

I have forgotten the reason, forgive me. I have forgotten my name in the language I was born to, forgive me.

My father did not beat us because he hated us. He beat us because he hated himself. I, in particular, terrified him, because I looked like him. And he did not want to be afraid or feared by his own children as he had feared his father. As an Indian man who still lived in lands that had been assigned to his tribe, then reassigned to those who stole them, he was belittled because he was feared. As a child I thought one of his names was *Chief* because that's what strangers and some of his friends called him. I remember sitting on his lap as my mother drove him from jail. He was still a little drunk and anger ricocheted back and forth between my mother and him. Outside the car the city was getting rich on Indian oil money that was now in the hands of white men. It was bright.

5.

The enemy immigrated to a land he claimed for his God.

He named himself as the arbitrator of deity in any form.

He beat his Indian children.

The law of the gods I claim state:

When entering another country do not claim ownership.

It's important to address the souls there kindly, with respect.

And ask permission.

I am asking you to leave the country of my body, my mind, if you have anything other than honorable intentions.

My father loved the water and the water loved him. The sun gleamed in every watery beautiful cell and he shined, attracted women with his sultry "good-looking Creek" looks. He met my mother and they danced until morning in that brand new city of oil and industry and soon there was marriage and four children, just like that, the world spins that fast. She was earth to his water, but nothing was enough to feed his hunger for the deep. He went fishing in the bars, the streets, until he offended the guardian of a lake by sleeping with his daughter. That was the end of any earth happiness. We lost him to the curse of the watermonster. And when he left our house the tentacles of the curse stung us, too. Our mother fled, married too quickly a stranger who beat us because he hated us. He threatened to kill us and burn down the house if she left and took us with her, or if I picked up the phone again when my father called.

6.

When the enemy went after my father he spared no weapon because he
wanted, he said, my father's soul.

But it was the land he was after—this beautiful land of harbor and sweet grass,
of palm tree and oak, of black earth, of red—

And we know that this earth cannot be owned by dictator or church, by cor-
poration or maker or signer of paper.

He took the land and moved all his relatives in. And when other immigrants
arrived from other lands he denied them what he had wanted for himself.

Though he wanted them for his customers.

The enemy made a circle of piss to claim us.

He cut everything down to make his cities and factories and burned

the forest to plant his fields. The wound so deep

it can be seen far above this blue green planet, far above us.

You cannot destroy a soul though you may destroy a planet.

You cannot destroy a song though you can make a people forgetful.

A soul can appear to be destroyed, and a song can disappear for a few gener-
ations only to reemerge from the heart of a child who turns and becomes a
woman.

We moved to a house on Independence Avenue with the man my mother married, a man who hated Indians. My mother said she married him because she didn't know how she would survive in those times, a woman with four children and no husband. I argued this with her when he left the house for work, but all she saw was a woman she knew who took her starving kids to an orphanage—and she didn't want that happening to us. So she worked and paid for everything. His money went into his savings. The house is still there, as evidence, and I cannot find it now even though I have driven up and down the street many times with the house number in my hand. In that house was a room filled with the man's guns, his jars of money and a piano. Once when the indigo sky lit up with falling stars, I got my brothers and sister up in the middle of the night to watch. We huddled there as refugees in his yard, taking in the blaze of promise and knew for a few hours there was something bigger than all of us that would eventually claim us, but like my father I kept forgetting.

7.

Spirits who watch over us are summoned to the point of impact, to any major collision to which they are assigned.

Did they walk with us through the rivers, the swamps, though we could not see them there at the edge of our heartbreak?

Where are you? my father asked the dark waters as he walked through the rest of his life without us. He said this to her, the daughter of the watermonster, not to us.

I was a teenager when I fled the house. I could not sleep at night because I had to protect myself from the enemy. Each dawn I finally dozed from exhaustion from the watch. When I left I carried everything in a trunk my mother bought me new at the army surplus store. I did not like leaving my brothers and sister to the mess but I was no use there against the enemy. Most bruises don't show but appear later in strange cities, or just as you wish to be clean and lovable to someone who is perfect. It will never work. You cannot change history. I kept looking back though I was safe at Indian school in another state. I kept looking back to see if I had forgotten something, to see if I could catch sight of my father in the glow of the city.

8.

We need a drink of water first, we tell the waitress who staples brown paper to the table at the seafood restaurant in these lands responsible for the delicate architecture of the marrow in my bones.

Backwards I fly, from Oklahoma, Arkansas, Mississippi and Alabama by plane, by the thread of a song shimmering in the sky.

By pure blood luck.

And suddenly I can see him over there, at the edge of the world, the swamp of seagrass and ghost crab, fed by the river of history. He's there, my father walking the brim, looking for her.

When a storm thunders miles out into the sea, the water in my blood is storming.

Oh, water trembling with light, if I think of you the enemy disappears into the deep.

I peered over the edge once and saw the souls of those who did not return from the deep. Many had leaped accidentally, led there on bad drug trips, others made a decision to lose their minds because the field of hurt was too painful and some were adventurous and then let fear clutch them to the wall. I turned back and walked through the living room to get away from the churning well. All that night I had been in the world of spirits, sent there on a chemical thread. I was shaken and the eye of the full moon hanging from the sky was scarlet with admonishment. The spirit is vulnerable and needs to be fed with tenderness and songs. It can be forced out by unspeakable violations of the body and mind, or by the spirits who live in the plants that are used in the manufacture of drugs.

9.

We sip our cool drinks in the world that is either flat or round, depending on the point of view.

Consider the world is neither flat nor round.

Think again. Think, said water, as it makes a house for my father.

Think, said fire as it reconstructs the nearest star.

Between them is a field of meaning in which there is no word for shame.

There is incredible depth to every grain of sand, to every nuance of creature, every gesture in the known and unknown universe.

Matter has converse weight in anti-matter.

Destruction and creation in the shell of a little house were father and daughter.

I try to appear as the savvy traveler, look smooth and inconspicuous in this new knowledge.

No matter, I said lightly, more to myself than to anyone. We will make it through this, past the edge of the wound.

When my children were babies and I bathed and oiled their beautiful bodies, I would squeeze them, kiss them and believed that nothing would contradict the words and songs I wrapped them in as I dried and held them close to me. Their diminutive kicks and squeals still delight me though they are grown with their own children now. Did my mother love me this way, and my father's mother love him this way and all the mothers in the world love their children like this? In that age, I still believed I could not be loved because I had failed, because my father left us, because no one protected me from the enemy, so how could my children believe my words when there was a contradiction between the waves and the deep? The incongruity made an undertow.

10.

I sweat. It's hot in this lush palace of earth and water.

We talk as if we were travelers anywhere in the colonized world, alert to tragedy and comedy.

We want to know if it's possible to separate and come back together, as the river licking the dock merges with the sea a few blocks away.

Long-legged birds negotiate the shore for food.

I am not as graceful as these souls.

I am vulnerable to your beauty, the fronds of seagrass tangling the wound.

I am invisible, and there is an emergency rising from the mud.

The baby's father never grew into a man; he is still a child stumbling in the dark. He's caught in time and he knows it, speared by the drama of his father who shot a lover and thought he killed her because he found her with another man. Then he turned the gun on himself. He died. She lived. And though it's been years his heart is still in third grade and cannot make it through the afterburn of violence. It's possible, I remember telling him, urging him so he would not kill himself and take my daughter and granddaughter with him. There is a map but you have to put down the beer, the hardstuff, the knife in your pocket. How do we carry all these stories on our backs? Maybe Kokopelli knew the trick. It had to do with music, a little singing as you walk the bloody cliffs between the sky and the earth.

11.

You are flushed from seawater and talking. Your style is radiant, and dignity is your hair falling exactly to your shoulders; your brown fingers have no doubt as to the ability to have what they want and need.

Your parents were gods who provided for you at any cost.

When you talk you weave a history sparkling bright with promise: a friend swimming the Mississippi with a bottle of wine in his teeth to catch up to the laughing crew, sunning nude in Provincetown, a friend you should have married and it would have lasted forever, the friend's father who mentored you and burned with the same flame that consumes you.

They all loved you without fail, without asking the question of your worthiness.

Your world is round and appears to gleam with perfection.

The elegant white heron on Kualoa Beach enjoyed the light winds and the smell of fish as we all watched the falling sun with reverence. I did not see guilt in his posture, nor did I hear him admonish himself for some failure of the deep or near past, rather he absolutely enjoyed his heron-ness, the wind, the sun and made note of the approach of the longest night of the year. He had no doubt as to his right to be a heron, or his right to enjoy the catch and taste of fish. But what do I know of herons? I do not know their language or their culture. We have human observations. Though for any small creature or god in this universe it comes down to attitude. You can walk through hell with your head up, still sparring with the fire, or you can be defeated by any small thing.

12.

I cling to your stories with my teeth, though I appear graceful, the winds off the water making my hair lift joyfully.

If I make your stories my life I will look bright in the new world.

I hold onto my paper plate stained with fried fish so it will not litter the river;

I hold onto my glass so I will not drown.

My eyes still blink with the force of the enemy's heels as he took down my father then headed for me.

I am trying to understand why the only story I can recall is drinking beer as a child on the beach of a man-made lake in Oklahoma.

I forget diving off the cliff into the water.

No one knows how deep or how shallow.

I feel nothing, hear nothing

It doesn't matter.

Nothing matters.

I see you there with rats in your hair and lipstick the color of night. It's your disguise in the world of lies and sweet pain, your signal that you are ready for love. You will know it when it descends the ladder of your teenage prayers uttered from your bedroom of confusion and dreams. You believe it has approached you in the shape of a boy you met in secret behind the Circle K, a stranger who gave you a little attention, a rough hello. There's a voice inside that urges you otherwise. There's the light that turned your room lighter than day. It's here in your heart, past the wreckage of broken families, and torn underwear. But you can't hear it, won't until you've walked through the hell of false love.

13.

I say nothing because my story appears to be about loss and failure.

I say nothing because I believed the story of the superiority of the enemy, with all his structures, his money.

I say nothing as a skiff of American tourists unloads at the dock with trailing, whining children.

I say nothing because they appear to have inherited the earth.

I do not like this space of nothingness.

It is not the nothingness of wisdom.

It is the nothingness of nothingness, stirring up the water until no one can see.

Prayers can be formed of words, clouds of thought or rituals of action performed with deliberation in the labyrinth. We prayed for my father who ran from his body as it choked for air as the sun began climbing the ladder after we had danced all night at the stomp grounds. We prayed thankfully because we had made it to this place and had plenty to eat of meat, potatoes and bread. The television continued to blare the news as the earth turned and turned. It didn't stop, nothing stopped, not the drama of human frailty or my father's spirit as it flew to the gulf waters lapping at the edge of the world. I made prayers over the confused body he left behind. The dank salt air that slowly ate his trailer made movement of song difficult but not impossible.

14.

Our paths make luminous threads in the web of gravel and water.

The shimmer varies according to emotional tenor,

to the ability to make songs out of the debris of destruction

as we climb from the watery gut to the stars.

Just ask the ghost crab who turns to stare as he walks sideways

through the kingdom of suffering.

He shrugs then disappears into the beautiful world.

There was a massacre in El Salvador. The soldiers had gathered all the men and boys in the church at the center of town and killed them. Then the women and the girls were taken to the fields and raped and killed. One particularly beautiful one was assaulted by many soldiers before they left her to die. She began her song as she was pushed down into the dirt and did not stop singing, no matter what they did to her. She sang of the dusky mountains who watched them that day from the clouds. She sang of the love of a boy and a girl. She sang of flowers and the aroma of the moon as it linked the night with dawn. She did not stop singing. She is still singing. Can you hear her?

Part III

This is my Heart;

it is a Good Heart

The Ceremony

All of my life I have entered into the ceremony from this door, toward the
    east into red and yellow leaves.
It has always felt lonely though there were always messengers, like the
    praying mantis on my door
when I opened it this morning. Or the smell of pancakes when there were
    no pancakes, coffee when there was no coffee.
I walked through the house we had built together from scraps of earth and
    tenderness, through the aftermath of loving too hard.
You were showering to get ready for war; I was sticky from late storms of
    grief and went to look for poetry.
Each particle of event stutters with electricity, binds itself to coherence.
    Like the trees turning their heads
to watch the human participants in these tough winds turning to go, as they
    continue to send roots for water making a language for beauty
out of any means possible though they are dying. Everyone is dying. I am I
    am, deliberately and slowly of this failure to correctly
observe the ceremony of letting go ghosts of destruction. I walk carefully
    through the garden, through the hallway of sobbing and laughter,
the kitchen of bread and meat, the bedroom of desires and can see no
    ghosts though they will take the shape of objects of ordinary living.
There is no poetry where there are no mistakes, said the next messenger. I
    am a human being, I said.

when I die

My band was performing two shows a day at the Cultural Olympiad at the 1996 Olympics in Atlanta when the bomb exploded near the stage we had played on just a few hours before. And as in any explosion the impact makes concentric circles of an infinite number out into the world. Everything changed. I went home and broke up a relationship. I was dying, I had been dying for a long time.

I walked back through the house we had made together of hopes and dreams, and as I gathered up my belongings to move out I made a ceremony for leaving. I went to every room and thanked it for the good times, for what I learned during the worst. I talked to the plants, smelled clothes and touched the things that would no longer be intimate to me. It was not easy and I had to stop within the circle many times.

I imagine when I die I will perform the same ceremony. My spirit, though anxious to leave the body of slow earth movement and pain, will turn briefly to acknowledge the husk it is leaving behind. And then it will go.

We Can See It with Our Eyes Closed

◉

You ask me what I am thinking when we make love
and our eyes are closed and the sun is climbing halfway
to the roof and the neighborhood dogs are all in love
with the spirit dog who makes the rounds and tortures them
with dreams of hills and running with the smell of heat
and then the train adds to the song of progress
making a web from city to city,
backdoor to backdoor and I know it is possible to
fly without the complications of metal and engineering
and all the payoffs, paybacks and terrible holes
in the earth and here we are in the territory of the wind,
surrounded by devils and thieves, forgotten by a trickster god
who has a wicked sense of humor
yet there is something quite compelling
about this skin we're in, a solid planet of gases and water
doesn't tell the whole story. I am intrigued by cloud
language and see you approaching as a red flower in a meadow
of yellow, or you are an apparition of rain just before or after
a famine of butterflies. We make an electrical reaction
like carbon dioxide, and did I remember to blow out
the candles lit for those who are dying and are leaving
or will leave this place? Grief is a land of wet tenderness. We are all
dying and will leave a trail like the plane jetting east in the direction
that becomes all directions, becomes all the millions of souls here together
looking for god or a little something to eat,
all of us blown away by the mystery of nothingness
as we shop in the streets for trinkets or bread.
We've been here before, thinking in skin and our pleasure
and pain feed the plants, make clouds. I see it with my eyes
closed. It's so beautiful.

traveling through the dark

I am a traveler. As a child my mother said all she had to do was rattle the keys and I would be the first one out in the car, ready for any adventure. We never went very far, mostly to the grocery store for staples of hamburger meat, oranges, and bread, or, when my mother got paid, to the hamburger stand that sold five hamburgers for a dollar. When my parents were together we'd go to the lake on the weekends in the summer. She'd get up early and make fried chicken and potato salad. My father would ice up beer and pop and we'd be off. These times I loved best.

I traveled at night into many worlds. Often as a child I found myself in the deserts of North Africa, the jungles of southeast Asia or wandering the neighborhood where I lived while everyone else slept and dreamed. I went on to make my living performing and have crisscrossed these lands many times. The ice horizon of Nome, Alaska, and the people there continue to call me back, as does my family on the Okanagan Reserve outside Penticton, British Columbia. I walked through clouds in Quito, Ecuador, and played saxophone with my band at the Piazza di Campidoglio in Rome as the sun turned everything golden. I have also walked through the war zone, witnessed families who were starving in the Mosquito Indian communities of Nicaragua. They weren't on either side of the war.

Flying is my preferred mode of travel, and there are many ways to fly I learned those nights I used to leave my physical body behind as a child. I also don't mind a small-engined plane as it tilts between the heavens and earth, the engine humming through your body like a song of praise for wind.

Another mode of travel is lovemaking which is similar to the travel of the spirit in dreaming; you bring your skin with you. Your skin is the map, the means through which you experience the transformation, the deep. You can skim the surface quickly, or you can dive through many layers into the deepest unknown territory of intimacy. It is there you will find the quivering raw essence of humanness, there at the center of power. This journey is fueled by the most powerful energy in this universe, an energy more potent than jet fuel or uranium or solar blast. It is called desire.

I always bring something back. Sometimes it is a little husk of fear, or a tendril of compassion. Once I saw how the energy looped back to feed the plants. Another time I had a lesson in the dynamics of volcanoes. God lives there.

Four Songs

1.

I fell through a hole in the sky from one end of the world
to the next. Burning off layers
like a comet
until I hit the surface of earth.
I awaken in a house on the edge of the Pacific
near a mango tree
with your sweet-smelling head
on my arm.

2.

The flower might appear vulnerable
as it bends with the tradewinds
drinks in the sun
the rain
but its roots extend to hell.
It keeps thinking: *beautiful.*

3.

What motivates us is mystery,
how the aloof stone desires more than anything
to be opened, shivering and wet with love.

4.

I didn't know how much I needed you.

reverence

Last night, in the middle of the night, I awakened into the jet stream of darkness. The surge of my life as it powered through dreams and history was pulsating, breathing. It was the midnight point of my awareness, as sleek as a panther, awakening me there in the middle of my life. I was afraid of the power of it; I was in awe. It is the same fear and awe that envelops me when I paddle on an outrigger canoe into the Pacific, or travel into the interior of myself and my beloved together when making love. I respect the gods there; I revere them.

Anniversary

◎

When the world was created wasn't it like this?

A little flame illuminating a rough sea, a question

of attraction, something fermented, something sweet?

And then a bird or two were added, the crow of course to

joke about humanity, and then another kind so beautiful

we had to hear them first, before our eyes could be imagined.

And it was, we were then—and there was no separation.

The cries of a planet formed our becoming.

We peered through the smoke as our shoulders, lips,

emerged from new terrain.

The question mark of creation attracts more questions

until the mind is a spiral of gods strung out way over

our heads, traveling toward the invention of sky.

Move over and let us sleep until the dust settles,

until we can figure this thing out.

What was created next is open to speculation or awe.

The shy fish who had known only water

walked out of the ocean onto dry land,

just like that, to another life.

Frog imagined meals of flying things and creatures in flight imagined hills

of daubed dirt and grass in which to settle and make others

to follow in their knowledge which they were building

as sure as houses on the tangled web.

And in that manner we became—elegance of fire, the waving grass.

And it's been years.

when my son was born

◎

Each anniversary involves a recounting of events. On my children's and grand-children's birthdays we recall the day they were born. Each year the stories grow more elaborate and detailed, and begin to have a life of their own. My son was born at the W. W. Hastings Hospital in Tahlequah (the old hospital, not the new one).

On the day my son was born I walked to the hospital with his father, carrying a small bag with diapers and baby clothes. We didn't have a car. (We eventu-ally got a car that we held together with tape and hope, but that was later, after we moved to Tulsa and got jobs cleaning at the hospital.)

When I was pregnant I walked everywhere, to buy groceries, do laundry or go to the library. Walking was my only mode of transportation, but it became my peace of mind. As I carried my son in my body I marveled at the evolutionary process taking place inside. This baby essentially began as a one-celled being, then transformed to fish, amphibian, a tailed mammal then a full-fledged human.

As I walked through that Cherokee town I wondered what would happen to us, where humans fit on the evolutionary scale. Were we truly necessary to the survival of the biosphere? For a biosphere like earth to thrive each life form must reciprocate the gift of life. What do we humans add besides stacks of trash and thoughtlessness?

No one noticed me as I lumbered through that town in my teenage body thrown off balance, as I stared in store windows dressed in homemade mater-nity clothes I cut and sewed from shirts and pants I owned that no longer fit. It was the first time in my life I was invisible, because I was heavy, and there was no shine from fresh fruit and vegetables.

And early that morning when I felt the first contractions announcing the ar-rival of birth, we headed to the hospital beneath a row of tall guardian oaks. I felt myself walking the path my mother's mother had walked, a Cherokee woman born not far from the old W. W. Hastings Hospital, which wasn't there when she or her mother was born.

This is all part of your story, I tell my son as we continue walking into the story, as dirt roads give way to asphalt, as children become parents, as nations fall apart.

A Song Travels the Arc Between Midnight and Sunrise

◎

You are sleeping under the dark belly of the night
as I am yawning while the sun cracks the sky
over Santa Maria.
So far away yet I still smell you in my hair and know that
I cannot forget you. Not in any part of the world,
no matter how beautiful the path under the fig tree
or the ripple of silver in the olives.
Later it will rain and the trees will stay up into the night
talking about it. All summer they were thirsty
and now they are exuberant and wet.
I drink perfect Italian coffee and eat grapes picked from the
arbor in the sunlight. My cousin fought in the war
in a field not far from here, enlisted and traveled
all the way from the Creek Nation.
Did he know any pleasure in this place?
The sun shines even when there is killing, though all life
trembles at any small cruelty.
Your spirit travels as you sleep, it is lighter than fear.
Have you made it past the plumeria tree,
over Moloka'i?
I think I am still dreaming
as I make preparations for the continuation of the journey
involving several principalities of water.
Where will we meet?
The water gods require praise and flowers.
Any song we make together will have to address them if we are to cross
from one nation to another by spirit, canoe or bird.
A young cloud of mist hovers
between your house and this refuge
in the memory of Tuscany.
It is willing to become the entrails of a song so fine
it will impress the guardians of water,

so beautiful it translates the distance
between desire and the intentions of the gods,
so powerful we travel the bow in the sky
safely to each other.

humans aren't the only makers of poetry

The young banana tree is making poetry; I see how it translates the wind. The need to make songs is inherent in all life.

I've watched plants hungrily drink rainwater. They are grateful and are more likely to sing if it is rainwater they are receiving. If it's water from a hose, they will drink it with gratitude but as they drink they keep looking toward the sky. And will eventually sing to bring the rain if they suffer from drought.

It's not just humans who sing for rain, make poetry as commentary on the meaning of life.

We aren't the only creatures, or the most likely to succeed.

This is My Heart

This is my heart. It is a good heart.
Bones and a membrane of mist and fire
are the woven cover.
When we make love in the flower world
my heart is close enough to sing
to yours in a language that has no use
for clumsy human words.

My head, is a good head, but it is a hard head
and it whirrs inside with a swarm of worries.
What is the source of this singing, it asks
and if there is a source why can't I see it
right here, right now
as real as these hands hammering
the world together
with nails and sinew?

This is my soul. It is a good soul.
It tells me, "come here forgetful one."
And we sit together with a lilt of small winds
who rattle the scrub oak.
We cook a little something
to eat: a rabbit, some oofkey
then a sip of something sweet
for memory.

This is my song. It is a good song.
It walked forever the border of fire and water
climbed ribs of desire to my lips to sing to you.
Its new wings quiver with
vulnerability.

Come lie next to me, says my heart.
Put your head here.
It is a good thing, says my soul.

earthly desire

In Kahali'i there is a place the Pacific loves to linger. It leans with sensual intensity against the land there, a lush and startling garden grown by the thoughts of the land as it fell in love with the water. Heading to the ocean is the Hanawi River dressed in flowers and bamboo who is also in love with the ocean. The story is complicated just as human stories can be complicated. The sky too is part of this story of attraction and yearning. The ocean and sky meet out on the horizon for the love of touch. To speak like this isn't simplification, or personification for the sake of making intimacy where there isn't— this is the truth of the matter. We are all here in this place because we desired it. Desired each other.

Protocol

I do not know your language though I hear the breaking of waves
through the vowels.
It is blue and if I am to follow protocol I will introduce myself
through my mother and hers until you know the liquid mass of ancestors
and in that you might know that I did not find myself
here on your island by some coincidence.
When you walk toward me from the ocean you are cobalt
and the people whose chants have constructed the intimate canyons of your
bones can be glimpsed suddenly as water clings to your skin,
your hair. I can hear the singing.
My spirit flew across the country of blue water
on a path made of a song that shifts the molecular structure
of rainclouds whenever it is recalled. Migration patterns form a network
of sense that mimics neuron patterns in the brain
of dolphins, water and humans.
When the Mvskoke emerged from that misty original place
we were led by four young winds, and a star who took the form
of talking fire. After we set up camp some of us went to look for water.
I found it years later, near the scarlet volcano just as it was predicted,
when companies of white men have fooled themselves and the sleeping
ones into thinking they've bought the world.
My family still has the iron cooking pot that was traded to us
when treaties were forced with blood. Those who signed were killed.
Now I have a gas range and there is no end to the war.
When I arrive from the sky after traveling through clouds
and the afterburn of jets I will consider the gift
of those who kept walking though their feet were bloodied
with cold and distance, as their houses and beloved lands
were burned behind them. I will consider the tyranny
of false rulers and how though they appear to dominate
your island they are small and brittle and will break.
When we meet at the gates of power you honor me with pikake and maile

and a chant that allows me to paddle with you into the waters
so I will not be known as a stranger.
I offer you coral and tobacco and a song that will make us vulnerable
to the shimmer of the heart, allows us to walk the roots
with our peoples through any adversity to sunrise.
This is how I know myself.
This is how I know who you are.

threads of blood and spirit

When traveling to another country it's important to recognize the spirits there, and acknowledge them with prayers, so that you won't inadvertently offend or hurt by ignorance of protocol of that place. Ask that your presence there is a blessing rather than a curse. Protocol translates as respect and reverence.

My first time in Hawai'i I went with friends to the place Pele lives on the big island of Hawai'i to make offerings. It had been raining through the night. Huge sheets of water pounded Mil's house on stilts and I thought for sure we would wake to major floods. If it were Oklahoma or Arizona we would. This was Hilo; we didn't, but still the rain hadn't stopped. We drove to make offerings in the downpour. The lava was running hot and we could hear Pele singing as the power of fire and water fumed, made clouds of hot mist that galloped to the ocean. Lava had closed a road leading to a black sand beach.

Mil told us the protocol of prayer. You open with a songline of ancestors by naming your mother, then her mother and all the way back. Most Hawaiians can go back generations. My Dakota friend, Sue, and I realized our prayers would be embarrassingly short. Neither of us could name very many generations. I know my mother's mother, her mother's name and hers and that is it. I can go further back on my father's side but still cannot name the concatenation of spirits that meet here in my body, my mind and spirit past a few generations.

We prayed, Sue, Mililani and I, though we were interrupted once by a man in a pack of tourists with cameras who wanted a photograph. Mil took care of him. She's often in this role of defending the sacred on her ancestral lands and I admire her fiery, brilliant spirit. Hers is a difficult path.

I used to relish my visits with my Aunt Lois Harjo, when we would drive through the Creek Nation to visit relatives and friends of her generation. When we drove to Okmulgee to visit our cousin George Cosar, Sr. they would speak Muscogee, then English intermittently for my benefit. This storytelling was a ritual of making a pattern of relatives, naming who was related to whom and the evolution of those lines of meaning until there was a web of intricate sense. Later I came to realize I needed this to make sense of my presence here as a Mvskoke person a few generations later.

Last spring I performed at the California Institute of the Arts for the students and was approached by a young native woman who gave me a note with which to introduce herself to me. It read in part:

Aatqa Audrey-nkuuq. Sivuqaghmiingunga. Pugughileghmiit ramkengitneng pingunga. Tapghalugenkuk Mekengankuk elltughaqagtegnenga. Asagumiinkuk Robert-nkuuq panikagttegnenga. Igaqughyuneghtunga.

My name is Audrey Powers and I am St. Lawrence Island Yupik. I am a member of the Pugughileghmiit Clan. I am the granddaughter of the late Don Uglowook and Doris Uglowook. I am the daughter of late Robert Powers and Ina Uglowook-Powers. I enjoy taking photographs.

I was honored and impressed protocol had not been lost or discarded as unnecessary in the post-colonial world. This introduction provides a thread of meaning that goes back generations, thousands of years, like the naming of ancestors in Okmulgee or Hawai'i.

Protocol is a key to assuming sovereignty. It's simple. When we name ourselves in this dignified manner then we are acknowledging the existence of our nations, their intimate purpose, insure their continuation.

Annunciation

for Desiray Kierra Chee

She is kicking, she is swimming
she is shining human laughter
        as she takes a turn
                upstream
her mother's dark crimson river.
She is stone, a fish, an answer
    to the question never asked.
She's the beginning and the end
            the river and the driven.
She's the baby, she's the mother
        the awe in awaken.
She isn't the first red star
            in this watery universe
nor will she be the last.
But she's the happiest
to accompany us—
As we learn to walk upright
and acquire the gift
of breathing
we catch the slippery laughing infant
delicately, with
        a net of heart.
Between the aaahhhs of creation
and the downstream of destruction
we make a home
where there
            are stars.

kinetics of wind

When I say this morning I felt my father in me I don't mean the obvious links of genetics: the eyes, hair, posture, shape of gesture. There was something else as I pulled on my pressed jeans, boots and white shirt then turned to walk by the mirror to see that it all fit. There's something like wind, how it is born from desire. It is an old desire, refueled by the need of life to expand and leap toward new knowledge, new forms. It defines muscle and bone, spirals through the blood, shaped by will and is the key to migration patterns in souls of many kinds, including humans, birds and whales. Each generation is a variation on the pattern. Eventually the pattern spirals toward a meaning that will reach to the other side of the sky.

When my granddaughter Desiray was born in Albuquerque, so quickly and relatively easily that the nurse said more babies would be born if all births were like this, and I held her for the first time, I noted, as any grandmother does, all the convergences of features in that small body. I saw my mother, the face she must have had before heartbreak. I saw the baby's maternal grandfather, and something of my aunt Lois whose spirit visited the room briefly to give this child a blessing. It's been my experience at the births of my grandchildren that someone who has gone on always visits, just after the birth has taken place or a few days later. Perhaps they are part of the whorl of the pattern and it draws them back.

Birth is one of the most powerful transformational moments of our lives. It is charged with the hopes and dreams of the parents, the relatives, and all other life that is connected with the event. Each event has a polar weight and at the presence of birth I have always felt death standing nearby. At death, birth too is a force that shimmers in the doorway. Ultimately death is a birth of sorts, just as the decay of sound begins immediately after the first cry.

I was standing in my daughter's living room with the baby in my hands, holding her after a feeding when she stretched and yawned. The muscles in my hands remembered the particular pull and spirit of my daughter, how she felt in my hands as I cradled her. I was holding her once again in the body of this new one, the same kinetics of wind harboring a huge spirit that would continue the loop of meaning that connected us. I wondered who before my daughter felt this way to her mother. Did I feel the same way to my mother as she fed me formula and put me to bed in the Creek Nation in Oklahoma? Or did my daughter's grandmother feel the same shape of spirit in her son, my daughter's father as she comforted him one summer morning just south of Mount Taylor?

Goodbye, arrivederci, ciao

for Laura Coltelli

Cara fig trees
Cara grapes in the arbor licked by sunlight
Cara blue sky
Cara crows who hold it up with their laughter
Cara the shepherd dog who walked with us the stone hills
Cara sunrise as it softens the dark streets of Pisa
Cara small winds as they toss the trash and leaves
Cara the dignity of small, unspoken kindnesses
Cara my friend's rich coffee in the morning
and cara olive oil in anything of meaning
Cara how I missed my island love here
Cara we are always traveling the songline of the heart
Cara this must be a favorite house of the gods
Cara heart of the earth I've held in my hands here
Cara my friend who once again drives me to the airport—
I'm always leaving and arriving
Cara those shining guardians who accompany us home
Cara cara

we never say good-bye

◎

Tuscany is a place in the world that sustains me. I know when I arrive there I will be taken care of, by the fig trees, the grapes, the sky, the kindnesses of the people, especially my friend Laura who is a guardian of my poetry. Some places in the world respond to us as an intimate relative.

In Cairo I felt I had come home, though it was far from anyplace or language that I knew in this life as a Mvskoke person from Oklahoma. I will never forget going to the famous coffeehouse with the poet Ali Darwish. A black cat with eyes of a yellow moon sat beneath the table for scraps. Ali Darwish fed him choice pieces from his plate. Beggar children came by selling tissues and other small items. He bought from each of them, they flocked to him because he loved them without question. This was beyond buying and selling. An elderly man came by with his box of polishes and rags. Ali Darwish had his shoes shined. Each act caused a shimmer in the labyrinth of suffering.

I learned about the source of poetry from him that night, more than I ever did in a writing workshop.

On the Saami lands in northern Norway I knew I could die and my spirit would be taken care of—how did I know that so absolutely that I could make a song of that thread of knowledge that would carry me through any storm, through fields of ice and snow?

In Hawai'i when I stood with Haunani-Kay Trask and Dana Naone Hall on the campus of the University of Hawai'i at Manoa as we were honored by a chant written and sung for us by Alika Kali, I felt the power of the words, his voice circle us and knew that there would be no good-bye in this place of good friends and beautiful aloha.

I have family over at Navajo, at Gila River, the Swinomish at LaConnor, Spokane, Ignacio, and Green Bay.

We never say good-bye.

The Gift

When I walked your land of buffalo and tall grasses
under a sky that shimmered thick with spirits who watched over you
I knew I had walked into an encampment of distant relatives.
Though it was winter, and your country is famous
for breaking horses and souls with little tolerance for ice and darkness,
I was taken in and seated next to the fire. The children were curious
about the songs I was carrying, the horn packed in the bag
that had traveled with me, many lands to get here.
You offered me soup with corn, and meat from a recent hunt.
We traded stories, laughter about the usual foul-ups of our terrible
human selves. We spoke quietly, even fearfully of the cruelty
galloping our lands, each new act of violence more inspired than the last.
We knew we knew nothing and this nothing was the huge expanse of mystery
kept alive in the brightness of remembering everything, from the exquisite detail
of the finest running horses, shining eyes of the newly born, or
spirits who allowed themselves to be kept in a song or story as food
through the longest seasons of brutality.
When it was time to leave we left behind any words of sadness
or hopelessness. I followed the tracks of other travelers
toward thinking stars on the horizon of loneliness.
I wanted you to know this song overcame me.
I carry you with me everywhere.

the design of light and dark

I was in Crow country when I was given the gift of a beaded key chain by a teacher there at the high school. She had watched me, she said, to see if I was really Indian, because I was light-skinned and a stranger and there are too many light-skinned strangers making the rounds of Indian country claiming to be Indian so they can sell their poetry, their music, their art. I understand her concern. I know I sometimes stand out on my father's side of the family, in the circles I travel in of Indian people, which puts me in a position to constantly have to prove myself. The tests are to be expected, and I know I am being watched more than someone else with darker skin. This hasn't made it easy for me in some communities. At a meeting in Ecuador an Indian woman with lighter skin than myself and Hispanic features tried to have me thrown out as a non-Indian. She didn't know me, nonetheless it was painful to be considered an intruder in a place to which I belonged.

One spring semester when I was at Indian school a girl showed up from Kansas. I believe she was of the Witchita tribe. Not only did she have it tough arriving after we'd all made alliances, she was model beautiful with green eyes and long light brown hair. The boys were after her big time, but many of the girls picked fights with her. They didn't for long, turns out she was the roughest of them all. She had to be to survive. Soon many of the girls who were her fiercest critics were her closest friends. They grew to respect her.

Lighter skin makes life easier in the white world. Those of us who are lighter are the reporters from the border, able to move stealthily, observe, then report back. I don't fit either world precisely. Mostly I am accepted in my community where I am loved and attacked as much as anyone else!

So I carried that beautiful key chain with its delicate design of light and dark as a talisman as I continued my journey. And everywhere I carried it I thought of the Crow woman and her dedication to the students, I thought of the students and their bright intelligence, their gift and love of poetry, I thought of the lush hills and how they met the immense sky, I felt the pull of spiritual mana in that place. That is the power of gift giving.

Morning Song

The red dawn now is rearranging the earth
Thought by thought
Beauty by beauty
Each sunrise a link in the ladder
The ladder the backbone
Of shimmering deity
Child stirring in the web of your mother
Do not be afraid
Old man turning to walk through the door
Do not be afraid

sudden awareness

There are images, songs and words that will appear at your death like famil-
iar birds to accompany you on your journey to the sky. They probably won't
be the most significant in terms of earthly accomplishment, and might even
embarrass you with their apparent meaninglessness or make you laugh at their
ridiculous appearance at a time demanding ceremony and grace. You will
hear the refrain of a stupid television commercial that aired years ago: "You'll
wonder where the yellow went when you brush your teeth with . . ." and it will
dance like a gnat just beyond reach, or some offhanded remark will insert it-
self just as you are searching the faces of your old relatives who have come to
greet you.

Sometimes I am suddenly starkly aware, caught by the sun shimmering
through the kitchen window as it slides below the horizon, or the shoulder of
my beloved as we turn to greet and everything matters, is suddenly perfect.
And I know instinctively these images rich with the power of light will come
back to me as I am leaving this place, will mark my sojourn here though these
moments may appear insignificant in the weight of memory.

It is early in the morning, still dark and frosty when I start up the truck to drive
to the airport in Albuquerque, refreshing to be out before the airwaves jangle
with the race. Once again I walk the windowed corridor after security to the
gates to catch a flight to somewhere in this eternal land, my horn in one hand,
my bag of poems and notes in the other. Then the sun rises up softly over the
Sandia Mountains and stops me there. I breathe deeply to take it all in, take
the sun and the mountains into my lungs. And I know that when I die it is this
moment that will surface, then go under, taking me with it.

Part IV

In the Beautiful Perfume

and Stink of the World

In the Beautiful Perfume and Stink of the World

◎

In these dark hours of questioning everything matters:
each membrane of lung and how wind travels,

I had been traveling in the dark, through many worlds,
the four corners of my mat carried by guardians in the shape of crows.

the french fry under the table the baby dropped,
my son grieving far away in a land of howling trains and enemies.

Above me was the comet, a messenger who flew parallel to my heart.
The speed of light translated my intimate life as seconds

Here loss is measured in tons, not ounces. And what-I-should-have-said
and what-I-should-have-done are creatures of habit

as a newborn star shimmering there, and then I stopped counting and
began to comprehend the view.

sitting on the bed, blocking my view of the sleeping moon.
If I get up to play my horn I'll awaken the neighbors.

My son was my dark-eyed baby again, kicking his legs after a bath,
and then he was a man with fire in his hands.

If I get up to pee I'll lessen my chances
of catching the wave of remembering and forgetting.

You can burn down my house, I said, or come over here and start a fire and
we will cook dinner and eat together.

So I waver here in the delicate traffic of cast-off ideas and doubt's antennae,
inside the wound of the perishable world.

And we did. And there were other trails through the dark; children began
killing each other and humans had forgotten

In the wake of gods who spiraled to earth unaware they were falling.
They fought and destroyed each other.

the promise to see the gods in any stranger who came to their door for food.
I found myself on the Nile in a felucca

Now we think we are left to our own devices, no one to slay the monsters
devouring us, no one to translate the din of the spin,

in the dark. In the boat were the poets, the philosophers, the singers, the
makers of new songs, those who could see past

of the wheels turning after the collision. The thread to the answer is in here
somewhere, a zigzag in a pattern of war and hunger,

the ordinary world. We convened here, beneath the night sky of the end of
the world, to reimagine the weave of the ladder

a thunderstorm carried on the back of a mountain
and we have been walking through fire forever to get here.

to the realm of all beautiful beginnings. It was getting late.
And the comet danced in the dark above us and we knew the comet was

To this room, to this night in which humans stir to the cry of a child
asking for water. To the sky bright with a traveler

the message and the messenger but we could not agree among ourselves.
We fought, then destroyed each other.

who drags a starry tail behind him flared with the wave of human need.
The comet palpitates the web with the heart's tentacles

And then found ourselves here again in the dark on the river of dreaming
as the new city built over the ancient crumbled around us.

brushes my head with its raw wandering, my shoulders, the roof of this place.
We are breathing in time through all of it, from

What is the meaning of all this? I asked, the wound in my heart
still quivering with the knife. And I heard nothing but the dark.

the terrified cling of marrow to teeth, to a lyric of beauty pushing
through wind. And it is all here. Everything that ever was.

The cawing, flapping song of the beautiful dark

In the dark. In the beautiful perfume and stink of the world.

—

Notes

Anishnabe—a North American tribe, also known as Ojibway and Chippewa.

beauty, beautiful—a Navajo (or Dineh) philosophical concept in which humans are recognized to be part of a harmonious system of thinking and being. The Hawaiians call this concept *aloha*.

cara—a term of endearment in Italian.

Crow—a North American Plains tribe.

hogan—a traditional Dineh home.

Ingrid Washinawatok—a Menominee activist who sacrificed her life while part of a humanitarian delegation to the U'wa people in South America. She and two others were killed for helping the U'wa people establish a cultural education system for their children to support the continuation of their traditional way of life. The U'wa people live in the Arauca Province of Columbia. The U.S. multinational oil corporations had been carrying out oil exploration in their home. The U'wa people had threatened to commit mass suicide if these oil companies were successful in the exploitative endeavors.

Israel Kamakawiwo'ole—a beloved Native Hawaiian singer whose songs continue to inspire at home and internationally.

Ken Sarowiwo—a Nigerian writer who protested the exploitation of his native lands by U.S. multinational oil corporations. He was killed by his government for his stance.

Kokopelli—the humpbacked flute player whose image is preserved in petroglyphs throughout the Southwest.

maile—a fragrant vine used to make leis for special occasions.

mana—spiritual power.

monster—There are three worlds in Muscogean cosmology: the Upper World, Middle World, and Lower World. The Lower World is rife with monsters, including the Watermonster who still occupies particular creeks and lakes in Oklahoma. Also refers to the monsters who roam this earth when humans set loose destruction by way of their negligence. Many of the earth formations came about because of the exploits of these monsters.

Mvskoke, Muscogee, Creek Nation—As a people we refer to ourselves as

Mvskoke. Muscogee is the English transliteration, and Creek Nation is the more generic term that came into use with European arrival in our nation.

Nusrat Fateh Ali Khan—a beloved singer from Northern India, trained in the art of Qawwali classical style. He made radical changes in his presentation of this art for contemporary audiences.

Okmulgee—the capital of the Creek Nation west of the Mississippi.

Pele—the female fire deity who resides at Halema'uma'u in Hawai'i.

pikake—jasmine flower.

plumeria—also known as frangipani, a fragrant flowering tree.

Pomo—a California tribe.

Saami—the indigenous peoples of Scandinavia.

smallpox blankets—blankets infected with smallpox issued by the government to Indian peoples as part of a genocidal policy.

sofkey—a traditional Mvskoke food of flint corn and lye.

tribal grounds—The Mvskoke Nation is divided up traditionally into tribal towns. The tribal grounds are the ceremonial grounds belonging to each town.

Vedic—relating to the Vedas, sacred Hindu texts.

Wichita—a North American tribal group.